Grace for the Injured Self

The Healing Approach of Heinz Kohut

Grace for the Injured Self

The Healing Approach of Heinz Kohut

TERRY D. COOPER

and

ROBERT L. RANDALL

PICKWICK *Publications* · Eugene, Oregon

GRACE FOR THE INJURED SELF
The Healing Approach of Heinz Kohut

Pickwick Publications
An Imprint of Wipf and Stock Publishers
199 W. 8th Ave., Suite 3
Eugene, OR 97401

www.wipfandstock.com

ISBN 13: 978-1-60899-839-5

Cataloging-in-Publication data:

Cooper, Terry D.

    Grace for the injured self : the healing approach of Heinz Kohut / Terry D. Cooper and Robert L. Randall.

    xiv + 162 p. ; 23 cm. Includes bibliographical references and index.

    ISBN 13: 978-1-60899-839-5

    1. Kohut, Heinz. 2. Self psychology. 3. Psychoanlysis. I. Randall, Robert L. II. Title.

BF109.K617 C75 2011

Manufactured in the U.S.A.

Robert L. Randall wishes to dedicate this book
to the congregation of St. Peter's United Church of Christ
in Elmhurst, Illinois, who, for over thirty-eight years,
embraced his counseling ministry with finances and affection,
and who even now graciously grants him use of his office
although retired from his duties there.

Terry D. Cooper wishes to dedicate this book
to Debby Hardesty, whose support, encouragement, and love
have helped sustain him through the writing of these pages.

Contents

Acknowledgments

Wе would like to thank Thomas Kohut for graciously and affirmingly granting us permission to publish the interviews with his father, Heinz Kohut. We would also like to express our appreciation to Charles Strozier, who supported our efforts from the beginning. We would also like to thank the late Don Browning, who was initially responsible for connecting us for the first time. Don was a mentor and friend to both of us and he is deeply missed. Terry Cooper would also like to thank Dr. Jule Miller, Dr. William Kelly, and Dr. Estelle Shane for significantly shaping his understanding of Kohut's work. We both wish to especially thank Dr. Arnold Goldberg for his generous time and encouragement of our entire project.

A single phone call between Cooper and Randall, who had never met, set in motion the project for this book. It has resulted in not only an extremely enjoyable collaboration between us, but in a warm admiration for each other. Each of us has found a new selfobject in the other that has blessed our self.

Greetings to Our Readers

W E TRY TO WARMLY greet everyone who enters into our academic classroom or counseling office. This is not a PR ploy. It is our attempt to provide a small grace-filled moment for others, the opportunity for them to feel recognized, to feel important, to feel connected so that they may be reassured, strengthened, and perhaps even healed.

Some people need that more than others. Our experience and training suggest, however, that every person struggles to some degree to hold their self together and therefore needs all the grace-responses they can get. And so permit us to extend our warm greetings to you as you enter into this reflective place.

This book is about the psychological injuries we all inevitably experience throughout life. Some of those injuries are mild, some are debilitating, most are in-between. This book is also about a new way to understand these injuries to our self, along with a new healing approach for dealing with them. We think you will resonate intellectually and emotionally with this fresh perspective on old problems. It is our intention to serve as coherent guides into this new way of understanding and responding. Moreover, we endeavor to illustrate how this approach, called "self psychology," can benefit that widest of ministries called "pastoral care."

These chapters, therefore, are not only for pastors, parishioners, pastoral counselors, church consultants, seminary teachers, and denominational leaders who try to be channels of healing grace; they are also for those injured ministers of grace themselves. All of us are included. Every individual, and every congregation, has suffered injuries to their self. Some have turned those injuries into blessings. Some have survived the injuries but are left with a limp. Some have been injured to near death; others to total collapse.

The perspective of self psychology was developed by the late Heinz Kohut. Kohut is considered by many to be the most important psychoanalyst since Sigmund Freud. His work has resulted in major changes in psychological thinking and clinical practice. Although one of the authors of this book has written extensively about Kohut and self psychology as it applies to church life, it is our joint assessment that Kohut's work is still basically unknown, and unused, by those in ministry.

We believe that Kohut's self psychology perspective uniquely illuminates how everyday people and groups construct their reality based upon the most essential motives and desires of their self. In addition to this interpretative framework, we believe that Kohut also provides a viable working attitude to take in helping individuals and groups restore their injured self. Kohut had no illusion of managing history, either of individuals or groups, but he did think that an informed, empathic understanding toward others and toward one's self, could make a crucial difference in the life of each. We are not attempting in these pages to train our readers to be self psychologists; instead we attempt to inform our reader about how self psychology can be, at the very least, a decisively influential background perspective for whatever they do in the broad work of pastoral care.

We also believe that Kohut's work can greatly aid our understanding of the dynamics of healing grace. Too often when it comes to the issues of brokenness, sin, acceptance, and salvation, some theological orientations can be what Kohut referred to as "experience-distant" rather than "experience-near." Grace, however, often occurs "horizontally," not just "vertically." On the horizontal, human side, grace is the act of embracing others with empathic understanding and empathic responses. "Empathy" is the shorthand term for empathic immersion into the self experiences of others by which we come to understand them, and for empathic responsiveness to their self needs shaped by our empathic understanding. As an act of grace, empathy is the most powerful means by which the self of an individual is reassured, strengthened, and even healed. Indeed, a case could be made that empathy is the foundation for all human acts of grace toward others. Being a channel of grace, therefore, entails freeing, exercising, and broadening our capacities for empathic immersion into the self experiences of others and for empathic responsiveness to their self needs.

While theology can certainly inform psychology, as Kohut distinctly affirms, human experience psychologically understood can also be a valuable resource for a vital theology. Our work, therefore, will attempt to show how self psychology's insights into injuries of the self can have important implications for the traditional understanding of sin, as well as for the relationship between empathy and grace. In the process, we will challenge some traditional conceptions of the human condition and invite our readers into an exploration of how the issue of self injury is pivotal for deepening our understanding of the human condition.

Finally, we believe that this book is important because it will introduce readers to very significant interviews with Heinz Kohut that had never been published before. Shortly before Kohut died in 1981, he accepted Robert Randall's request to interview him. Kohut graciously invited Randall into his home for two lengthy interviews dealing with Kohut's self psychology understanding of the role of religion for individuals and for culture. These interviews were granted in part because of Kohut's familiarity with Randall's extensive attempts to bring pastoral counseling into dialogue with self psychology. The interviews elaborated on some of Kohut's perspectives that had only been touched on in his earlier writings. They are compellingly positive for the role of religion in maintaining self cohesion throughout life and in restoring cohesion to selves that have been injured.

Randall has gained full permission from Thomas Kohut, the son of Heinz Kohut, to publish these interviews in whatever form he deems best. Thomas Kohut, in fact, remembers his father speaking favorably about Randall's interest and work. This book contains complete transcripts of those interviews.

Here is how we will proceed. Chapter 1 offers a friendly introduction to Kohut's perspective and the basic tenets of self psychology. Chapter 2 then examines Kohut's conviction that injuries to the self represent the central problem of the human condition. This chapter places Kohut's position within a broader framework of Western perspectives about human nature. We employ a self psychology perspective to look afresh at theological ideas that may restrict our empathy for our self and for others.

Chapter 3 shows how self psychology understandings are relevant to the traditional Judeo-Christian concept of sin, and especially the seven deadly sins. It explores how sin related to injuries to the self.

In chapters 4 and 5, we shift our focus to how self psychology can benefit our understanding of grace in pastoral care activities. Chapter 4 follows an actual minister through one of his actual days and reflects in depth on his many pastoral encounters from the self psychology perspective. In chapter 5 we use the self psychology perspective as a tool for providing pastoral counseling guidance for three churches that are "fragmenting" in three different ways.

In chapters 6 and 7, we provide two interviews with Kohut that have never before been published. These interviews, conducted by Robert Randall, reflect Kohut's views on religion and its value in addressing psychological needs. Chapter 6 contains the interview conducted on March 22, 1981, while chapter 7 contains interview from April 12, 1981.

Then finally, in chapter 8, we each reflect on the significance of Kohut's comments on religion in his interviews. We look at the contributions Kohut makes to the understanding of religion, to the working alliance between religion and self psychology, and to the lives of religious believers and religious seekers.

The 32nd Annual International Conference on the Psychology of the Self met in Chicago during the third week of October 2009. We authors were there. The title for that conference was "The Forward Edge of Self Psychology." Part of that "forward edge" was to emphasize again a forward edge Kohut had established years before: the crucial and indispensable role of empathy for others as the primary means by which persons are reassured, strengthened, and even healed. We agree. We know this not only intellectually but personally. It is our hope that we can make this perspective abundantly clear in the pages that follow, and might, thereby, contribute grace-moments for parishioners, congregations, and for those who serve them.

Terry D. Cooper
Robert L. Randall

1

The Self Psychology Perspective

NEW CREATIVE ENDEAVORS DEEPLY engage three aspects of the innovator's life: their thought, their work, and their person. These three are interrelated yet separate domains. It is possible to "read" Heinz Kohut in these three ways. One way is to look at his thought. This has to do with the ideas and conceptualizations at the heart of his self psychology. Another way is to look at his work. This involves a consideration of his self psychology as a treatment approach for those suffering from disturbances of the self. A third way is to look at his person. This focuses on the imprint Kohut has left on self psychology that gives it a distinctive cast. We intend to present the self psychology perspective in these three ways.

THE BASICS OF SELF PSYCHOLOGY

You already know a lot about the "self" that Kohut talks about. You know it implicitly, through your experiences. You probably have used different words than self psychology uses, and you may not have consciously known the broader importance of the self as revealed by Kohut. But you are a self, and you already have an in-the-bones understanding of your self. We begin with that.

As you sit reading these words, it would be peculiar for you to say, or to acutely feel, "I am these hands holding this book," or "I am these eyes scanning these words." As individuals we exist through our body, yes, but we sense being more than our body parts or body processes. In the same way, you do not ordinarily say, "I am these thoughts going on in my head." You experience your self as more than just mental processes, more than just what you are thinking at the moment. Similarly, in normal living you do not exist in a state of depersonalization where you feel that all you are is the role you play. That may happen from time to time, as all of us know, yet we typically experience that there is more to us than the performance of roles.

You implicitly know that there is this more inclusive dimension to you, something that holds all the parts, processes, and roles together. We typically refer to this core as our "self." It is natural for us to sense and refer to our essential personhood as our "self," by which we indicate the central structure and wholeness of our being. The points are these: first, without being taught it you sense that you are a self; and second, you also sense that your self is the nucleus, the core, of who you are.

There's something else we implicitly know. The state of our self—its level of assuredness, its sense of well-being—is subject to fluctuations. Sometimes we feel alive and full of zest. We have energy for our own ambitions; we feel uplifted by our ideals; and we have deep empathy for the needs and struggles of others. Indeed, at moments we feel like singing, "I'm sitting on top of the world!" At other times we may feel depressed and limp. Projects and values seem empty, and our capacity for empathizing with others is depleted. It is then that we are inclined to sing the mournful spiritual, "Nobody knows the trouble I've seen."

Hopefully you do not regularly swing back and forth between these extremes, but you know, implicitly, what those extremes are. And you know that all of us experience some fluctuations in the firmness of our self. We know this is normal, but we are also aware that some people seem able to maintain a generally positive feeling about their self even during stressful times, while other people feel their self threatened by nearly everything. To say it more precisely, we know persons who experience their selves as firm and consistent, who have positive and reliable self-esteem, whose body, mind, and emotions are balanced and harmonious. We know other people who experience their self as shaky and always on the verge of falling apart, whose self-esteem is unsteady and easily injured, and whose emotional, physical, and mental activities are listless, excessive, or in conflict. The first group has what self psychology calls "firm self cohesion." The second group has what self psychology calls "weak self cohesion."

There are varying degrees of self cohesion between these two extremes, of course. Hopefully your self has developed so that you feel basically strong and resilient. If so, then you tend to bounce back to some healthy state of self cohesion after encountering blows to your self (which self psychology calls "self injuries") rather than experiencing your self falling apart to some degree (which self psychology calls "fragmenting"). The point here is this: not only do you implicitly sense you have/are a self and that it is the center of who you are, you also know that the condition of the self fluctuates between a general state of cohesion and a general state of disequilibrium.

What brings about this fluctuation in the self? Why do we sometimes feel so great and other times so lousy? The answer has to do with how responsive we feel others have been to us and how responsive we feel they presently are. We experience that in three main ways.

- When we experience others approving of and applauding us we feel confident inside. Over time our self-esteem builds up from these affirming responses of others so that we are able to healthily affirm our own values and goals and self-perceptions.

- When others are reliably available to us to lean on when the going gets rough and we are upset, we feel calmed and fortified inside. As a result of being responded to and feeling merged with uplifting individuals, we become able, over time, to soothe our own self when we are alone or hurt.

- When others typically convey to us that they are like us and we like them, we feel that we belong, that we are included, that we are connected to others in deeply meaningful ways. As a consequence of being responded to by people who demonstrate that they are like us and we like them, over time we grow in the capacity to assure our self that we are normal and acceptable.

What wonderful, life-giving experiences these are! They are the essential experiences necessary for the development and maintenance of a cohesive, balanced, and vital self. For some of you these experiences are so naturally present that you take them for granted. Blessed art thou, for these are the roots of your basic sense of well-being in life. Others of us whose self is chronically shaky may not have known specifically what was absent in our life, but we have been painfully aware that something critical was missing.

From childhood on we have learned in our bones that how we feel and respond is in large measure influenced by how we experience others being for us. Self psychology gives the term "selfobjects" to those whose empathic responses we need for the development and well-being of our self throughout life. Sometimes we have an intense, urgent need for people to empathically respond to us so that we can hold our self together. And we may do whatever is necessary to get those responses. At other times we have a more quiet need for people to respond to us so that we can continue to feel adequate. The crucial point is that the fluctuations in our self cohesion are the results of how we experience others affirming or disconfirming us.

Something else happens to us when we feel let down by persons we rely upon to help us feel good about our self. When we are criticized or disappointed or rejected, we tend to respond by drawing back or by striking out. Injuries to the self lead us to withdraw in hurt or to react with rage. There is a wide range of depressive-withdrawal responses: from mild dismay to deep melancholy marked by grave self-doubts and even suicidal thoughts, for example. There is also a wide range of rage responses: from passive-aggressive acts to obsessive efforts for revenge, for example.

Although the world frequently does not seem to understand, we know inside that our withdrawal and/or rage are often our ways of trying to hold our self together. When our self is injured, we do all we can to feel reassured inside. Sometimes we do that by pitying ourselves; sometimes by getting hopping mad.

There are many other ways in which we strive to regain our self cohesion when we are injured. A person might attempt to reinstate self-esteem by remembering how he was affirmed as special by persons in the past. Or, a person may engage in some creative or physical activity that reaffirms physical and mental strength. Or, a person may immerse her self in comforting communion with God. Then again, we may engage in showy, impulsive, even risky behavior as ways to ward off terrible feelings of emptiness or uncertainty. The points to be made are these: we recognize how we search for empathic responses from others so that we can feel safe and strong; we also recognize our active efforts to restore and preserve our self cohesion when it is disturbed.

In our rich storehouse of implicit knowing is one final gem we want to unpack, namely the central needs of the self. We have already alluded to them.

1. From the time when we were small we can remember how the applause and words of praise from others made us feel really good about our self. Eventually those affirming responses built up and lodged within us and became the basis for our positive self-esteem throughout life. As a result, we are now able, as grown-ups, to be motivated and supported by our own mature ambitions and plans, and are able to still feel good about our self even when we fail at something, or when, alas, others criticize us.

If you think about it, however, you realize that you the grown-up, with the blessing of secure self-esteem, still want those experiences of being recognized, made special. You sense that you still need "mirroring" responses, as self psychology terms them: those responses of admiration and praise that keep you feeling confident. While hopefully you may not need mirroring responses in the same intense form you did as a child (mother jumping up and down applauding when you learned how to ride a bike, for example), you still rely upon more mature forms of mirroring for your ongoing, inner sense of well-being (dignified but appreciative applause after you give a speech, for example).

We do not outgrow mirroring needs; we just need them in more mature forms—if, that is, our self cohesion and self-esteem have originally been made strong by empathic responses in our growing up. If we have not been adequately mirrored by our early selfobjects, our self will fail to reach its full maturity. We will still operate out of our childhood grandiose self that needs, if not demands, mirroring responses to whatever we do or say. You see these traits in others; you may have some your self. Here our self is still needy, still vulnerable, still not firm, still in need of others to give us that assurance that we are special which we cannot give to our self. That's a very difficult position to be in. Kohut helps us understand that we need to have deep empathy for those who try to hold their self together by seeking mirroring applause for their often obnoxious behavior.

2. Similarly, we can sense how from the beginning we have needed strong comforting figures to run to with our tears and bruises when we have fallen down. We can remember how the reassuring words and actions of Mother or Dad soothed the hurt when kids picked on us and gave us the courage we needed to go back and try again. Those empathic responses over time became part of our own ability to regulate our internal tensions

and to soothe our own self. Consequently, as mature grown-up selves we are now able to find inspiration through our own ideals and values that lift us up. Furthermore, we can find encouragement in the memory of empathic responses from idealized persons in our past, and can experience joyful satisfaction from knowing that we share the visions and values of admired individuals we have never met. In this secure self state we are energized to present our self as a source of peace and strength for others, doing for them what has been done for us.

Have we outgrown this need for "merger" responses, or "idealizing responses," as self psychology terms them: those responses from idealized, uplifting individuals in whose embracing presence we feel assured and whose courage we borrow for our own? What does your heart say? It says we have not outgrown them. If our self cohesion has a firm foundation, then we won't need idealizing responses in the same form we needed them as a child. We will no longer need to sit in Dad's lap and have him stoke our head as he comforts away our fear. Instead, we may feel a comforting glow by remembering his calm demeanor and the wisdom he imparted to us. But we never outgrow the necessity for reassuring responses from individuals we maturely idealize.

If, however, our life was void of idealized figures to merge with, or the responses of our idealized figures hurt us more than soothed us, then our self may not have adequately matured. We will still operate out of our childhood idealizing self, needing to feel an intimate part of individuals and groups we declare are great and powerful and "the best." Only then can we feel safe. Only then can we feel any sense of calm certainty. This, too, is a painful situation to be in. As Kohut helps us understand, people will do nearly anything to escape the ravishing fears within them over which they feel powerless.

3. Finally, we can also recall those actions and words from important persons, inside the family and out, who conveyed to us that we were not weird, not an outsider, but just like them and they just like us. How wonderful it was to feel that we belonged and were not left out! If we were fortunate enough in our early years to experience reliable responses that assured us that we were included by self-same others, or that they were in essential ways almost like our twin, then our self matured in this area. As a consequence, we do not worry so much about "fitting in" because we have a deep conviction—often unrecognized—that we are the included

kind. We are also able to enjoy shared activities and to cultivate occasions of togetherness. In addition, we possess the ability to feel an abiding and broad sense of belonging: not just to our family or friends or colleagues but to the whole of culture, to the whole of one's generation, even to the whole of humanity.

Have we outgrown this need for "alterego" responses, as self psychology terms them: those responses from others that assure us we that we are normal and acceptable? Implicitly you know the answer is no. They, too, along with mirroring and idealizing needs, are a normal part of us, present when we were children and present with us now as grown-ups. If our self has matured, that is, has developed reliable self cohesion and self-esteem, then we will not need alterego responses in the form we did as a child. We will not still need those around us to dress and think and act just like we do, as a kind of copy of us, in order for us to feel connected to others. Instead, an assured sense of connectedness may be reconfirmed as we say with alike-enough others the prayer Jesus taught us.

However, if we have suffered from absent or weak alterego responses to our need for inclusion with self-same others, then this aspect of our self remains stuck with its childhood yearnings. Our self does not mature adequately; it does not achieve reliable self cohesion and reliable self-esteem. We still hanker for those who will mold themselves to be just like us, either in essential ways or in identical ways. While we search intensely for places to belong, we are quick to reject any person or group whose looks or speech or dress does not match our own. We are supersensitive to being disappointed by those we thought shared our mind and outlook on something, especially if we have expected them to be a comforting echo of our own self. This, too, is a painful situation. Kohut helps us understand that when an individual suffers from not feeling included, not feeling like others, and not feeling normal, they may then desperately do anything that will assuage this pain of isolation.

One last realization: Every one of us, even the most self-secure, even those with highly empathic selfobjects in our past, can lose our self cohesion and begin to fragment to some degree when burdens and injuries become too heavy. Every one of us can regress to those childhood ways of needing intense mirroring, idealizing, and alterego responses. Hopefully that is only temporary until our self regains its equilibrium. In the meantime it can be a harrowing journey until that happens.

Perhaps we can now begin to accept these narcissistic/self needs as part of who we are. Maybe we can even accept them wholeheartedly rather than begrudgingly. To do that is to move toward fuller empathic understanding of this lived reality we call our "self."

THE THERAPEUTIC WORK OF SELF PSYCHOLOGY

Kohut's self psychology insights developed out of his many years of psychoanalytic work with patients in analysis with him. Some of these patients were struggling with problems of conflicting drives, which the psychological literature called, in general, "neuroses." For these drive-conflicted difficulties, the traditional psychoanalytic approach, which focused on drives and defenses against drives, was considered the appropriate treatment method.

But Kohut also worked with another type of patient, those struggling with problems of "narcissism," as the psychological literature generally defined them. This type of patient was characterized by a specific vulnerability: his or her self-esteem was unusually unstable, and, in particular, he or she was extremely sensitive to failures, disappointments, and slights from others.

Psychoanalysts and psychologists had long observed these narcissistic characteristics in some of the people they treated. The analytic approach called "classical psychoanalysis," which closely followed Sigmund Freud's formulations and methods, considered a narcissistic individual to be fixated at a primitive phase of development referred to as the "auto-erotic stage." Briefly stated, the individual was considered self-absorbed, involved more with self-love than with love for others (thus the term "narcissism" after the figure in Greek mythology, Narcissus, who fell in love with a reflection of himself in a pool and was unable to love others). Normal psychic development meant, for traditional/classical psychoanalysis, that an individual would eventually pass through and basically relinquish this early narcissistic, self-love stage in the process of forming solid "object relationships." At this advanced developmental stage other persons would be experienced and related to as "objects," separate from the individual's self, but to whom, in the forming of "object love" ties, the individual would become emotionally invested rather than remaining invested in the individual's autoerotic self.

This understanding of narcissism determined the treatment of persons stuck in this stage of self-love. In short, there was no treatment. Traditional Freudian psychoanalysis believed that narcissistically bound individuals *could not* be treated by psychoanalysis since, being so focus on their self (self-love), and not sufficiently able to relate to others in an object-relations way, they were unable to form a transference relationship to the therapist, which was considered the prime means for analytic cure.

As Kohut worked with "narcissistic" individuals, however, the formulations of classical Freudian psychoanalysis did not seem to fit what he was experiencing. In the first place, Kohut found that these individuals *could* and *did* form a particular type of relationship to him in the therapy setting. A transference *was* established. A person with narcissistic problems (whom Kohut later referred to as suffering from a "narcissistic personality disorder," later changed to "self disorder") would emotionally respond to Kohut as if Kohut were inseparable from the individual's very self. The patient made Kohut a psychological extension of the person's own inner world, where Kohut was expected to function in ways the self needed, and at times, demanded. Kohut felt himself no longer engaged as a person in his own right (a separate object), but as one whose existence now was to be responsive, indeed, perfectly responsive, to the self of his patient. As Kohut came to name it, he had become the person's "selfobject," an object only insofar as he was connected to the person's self.

Kohut's narcissistic patients were not psychotic. They did not generally hallucinate or lose touch with reality. They knew Kohut was a real person, that his education was different from theirs, that he had his own family of which they were not members. Nonetheless, the essential psychological nature of their human relationship was the appropriation and experience of Kohut as an extension of their self, as their selfobject.

Kohut quickly realized that such person's self was very vulnerable. Psychologically they lacked centeredness and cohesion, lacked firm self-esteem, lacked the ability to function with balance and harmony, and lacked the capacity to keep their anxieties and angers in check. Because they suffered from inadequate psychological capacities necessary to sustain their own mental, emotional, and physical equilibrium, these persons needed Kohut to respond to them in reassuring, affirming, and soothing ways. The vulnerable, easily fragmented person needed either "mirroring," "idealizing," or "alterego" selfobject responses, as Kohut eventually understood and named the particular types of relationships (transferences) that persons eventually established with him.

Kohut began to realize that this ebb and flow in a patient's self-esteem and self cohesion—as Kohut either adequately fulfilled his particular selfobject role or failed in it—were re-dramatizations of traumatic selfobject responses from the patient's past. Persistent narcissistic needs not met by unresponsive or unavailable parental selfobjects were played out with Kohut and others again and again.

How then did one interpret what was happening with these individuals suffering from self disorders? Did the traditional perspective of Freudian psychoanalysis seem to fit, which held that the person was fixated at a primitive stage of development and could not be treated and could not be healed? In the face of all that he had been taught as a classical psychoanalyst, Kohut said no.

Kohut observed and then articulated a new perspective in which the history of the self's empathic relationships was as crucial for the development of a person as the history of the person's psychosexual drive experiences. That is, Kohut posited that narcissism is not disposed of on the way to the development of object relations. Instead, narcissism has its own separate line of development: from immature selfobject needs to mature selfobject needs, in the same way that there is development from immature object relations to mature object relations. More than that, Kohut began to see that not only does narcissism not go away, and not only does it have its own line of development, but that it is also the psychological bedrock of all life. The primary way in which individuals engage each other and approach things in the world is through making them selfobjects. The central psychological relationship is one that Kohut called the "self-selfobject relationship."

But finally, and perhaps more an occasion for grace than anything else, Kohut found and articulated a therapeutic approach in which the vulnerable and fragmenting self could be restored. When the person's narcissistic needs and history of selfobject traumas were empathically considered; when Kohut let himself become an empathically responding selfobject figure; and when Kohut empathically interpreted to his patients the meaning of their narcissistic yearnings and their reactions to selfobject failures, then gradually the person began to experience having a stable sense of self and a stable state of self-esteem. More and more such persons were able to keep their self together rather than have it fragment to some degree when they felt injured by others. Slowly their narcissistic rage and/or their depressive withdrawal lessened as they began to employ new ways to handle the tensions that arose within them when their selfobjects failed to function as they wanted. In short, Kohut's new self psychology work had resulted in new possibilities for the healing of the injured self.

THE IMPRINT OF KOHUT'S PERSON
ON SELF PSYCHOLOGY

Self psychology is more than a body of clinical thought, more than a particular therapeutic approach. It is also a value system. Those values come from the person of Kohut. This in itself is not peculiar. Kohut is very clear that "There is no science of man that is thinkable without some value system behind it."[1] But what is remarkable are the subtle—and not so subtle—ways in which Kohut expands both the role and the value of self psychology and its viewpoint. These role and value expansions are not disconnected from self psychology as a body of thought and as a clinical approach, but they are not logical, inevitable extensions of Kohut's original self psychology insights into the development and cure of the self. They emerge from Kohut himself, from his personal reframing of self psychology's role and value in human life. A psychologist or psychoanalyst could generally accept Kohut's developmental interpretations and clinical techniques but leave out the elevated role and value-laden ethos with which Kohut eventually casts the role of self psychology.

Stated in self psychology terms, but in a folksy way, self psychology became Kohut's selfobject baby. After a hard gestation period, in which some in the traditional psychoanalytic field chastised him for getting pregnant with alien ideas, and after a hard delivery, in which he was rejected by some admirers once close to him for actually giving birth, Kohut began to delight in the unfolding of his self psychology perspective. He took enormous pleasure watching others begin to admire his selfobject baby. He was deeply gratified when others offered, even competed with each other for the chance, to nourish this new analytic infant.

Kohut knew his selfobject creation would eventually, and appropriately, begin to have a life of its own—and it still has. Self psychology as a general movement has gone in many different directions. But Kohut was also intensely protective of his selfobject baby. Especially in the last decade of his life he strived to infuse it with certain roles and values that would endure no matter what form it took. He expected his selfobject creation to grow up and flourish, but he wanted it to always retain certain elevated purposes and aims.

We do not intend to present a psycho-biographical study of the origins of Kohut's self psychology. What we now do is simply lift up three areas that indicate how Kohut engaged in the process of role and value expansion. The insertion of Kohut's own person via his expanding role and value efforts is part of the whole ensemble we have called the "self psychology perspective." Understanding self psychology involves grasping this dimension of its makeup.

Empathy as the Way to Be in the World

From the time that Kohut delivered his first paper on empathy at the Psychoanalytic Congress in Paris in 1957, he highlighted empathy as a means of investigation and data collecting.[2] In fact, he considered empathy the only valid method for gaining psychological access into the subjectivity of another person. To understand the outer world, we use the methods of extrospection, such as microscopes, telescopes, and other mechanical methods of measuring the external world. These are completely appropriate means for investigating external reality. When we focus on the inner world of a person, however, these various forms of extrospection are not appropriate for the task. For Kohut, psychology is the study of complex emotional states, and empathy is the only appropriate data-gathering tool that helps us vicariously experience and adequately interpret the experiences of other selves. Indeed, only material gained via this empathic immersion method can be legitimately called "psychological."

Of all the subjects Kohut could have addressed in the final presentation of his life, he chose to come back to the topic of empathy. The occasion was the 1981 Self Psychology Conference.[3] Kohut, who was dying of cancer, gathered strength and courage to speak to his colleagues and followers one more time. He died four days later. Kohut declared that he had chosen the topic of empathy precisely because it had been so confused in the minds of many people.

Perhaps so. But perhaps Kohut needed to reaffirm that empathy was not sentimentality or sympathy, but a research tool for entering into the subjective life of another, *because Kohut himself was responsible for much of that confusion.* Over the years Kohut had intentionally expanded the meaning and role and value of empathy to the point where empathy as a research tool had become somewhat lost or minimized. Kohut, however, did not entertain that as a reason for why people might have been confused about empathy.

As we have noted, Kohut began his self psychology work by defining empathy as an epistemological, scientific mode of research. Empathy was "vicarious introspection," the process in which we put ourselves in the other person's shoes and then try, through consulting our own resonating feelings and through using thought experiments, to decipher the inner world of that other. From early on, empathy became for Kohut the *means* for accessing the inner life of others. There was no other entry. Indeed, for Kohut empathy was also the *determiner* of psychological data. Only that material gained through the empathic-immersion method could be considered "psychological."

But Kohut moved beyond this, expanding the role and value of empathy. Although in that final public presentation in 1981 he expressed great reluctance in having to admit his belief that empathy has a "therapeutic effect—both in the clinical setting and in human life in general,"[4] this was a somewhat disingenuous admission. Throughout his writings Kohut wove the theme that healing comes from the life-giving experience of feeling connected to those who empathically understand us. Grace for the injured self does not come, for Kohut, from what we might call a "corrective cognitive experience"—from new knowledge about psychological reality and consequent living according to that knowledge. Neither does restoration of the self come basically through a "corrective emotional experience"—experiencing true love; establishing trust, for example. And neither does cure of the self come through a "corrective actualizing experience"—forming a solid identity, achieving independence, becoming individuated. Finally, neither does healing come through a "corrective moral experience"—doing one's duty; abiding by values and ideals, for example. Healing comes when a person feels empathically understood. Then it is that insights help us along; then it is that we are open to new emotions that enhance our living; then it is that self-actualizing efforts become efficacious; then it is that new moral imperatives uplift and sustain us. It is empathy that cures.

The point is that Kohut expanded the meaning, role, and value of empathy. Empathy is more than the *means* for psychological investigation, more than the *determiner* of what is and is not psychological material. It is the *agency* by which souls are restored. It is the glue that holds a broken person together until they begin to heal, and then it becomes the nourishment that keeps them going, keeps them striving to live fully and vibrantly. Kohut expands the role of empathy and gives it elevated value.

But Kohut expands empathy's role and value beyond this. Kohut makes empathy a mark of maturity, perhaps even *the* mark of the ultimately healthy self. A person whose narcissism has been successfully transformed into the highest forms of self-expression will exhibit capacities for deep humor, true joy, and penetrating wisdom. Although Kohut says that man's capacity to acknowledge the finiteness of his existence "may well be his greatest psychological achievement",[5] in most of Kohut's work the mark of a mature, transformed self is the ability to live each day with broad, encompassing empathy for others and for one's self. Humor, joy, wisdom, and acceptance of death become certified, as it were, as they become expressions of an empathically filled individual. Being able to respond empathically becomes implicitly as well as explicitly the standard of health for individual and group selves, on which those in the practice field should keep their eye. Indeed, it may even be plausible to say that for Kohut responding empathically is also the *moral obligation* that should be espoused by all concerned because it fits best into the specific self needs Kohut deems of ultimate significance in our culture.[6]

There is more. Even beyond this Kohut envisioned empathy as the *essence* of humanity, as the essential humanizing power we possess. Empathy is more than the *means* for psychological research tool, more than the *determiner* of psychological data, more than the *agency* for therapeutic cure, more than the *mark and standard* of psychological health, more than the *obligatory behavior* we should practice as the model of social conduct. Empathy is elevated as the *essence* of the human spirit.[7] What it means to be human is to be empathic. Only via empathy are we truly human. Indeed, one can sense in Kohut that empathy is also the *hope* we have for the biological and spiritual survival of humanity.[8]

Those who want to utilize the self psychology perspective may not be swayed by this expanded role and value of empathy. Empathy may be taken merely as "one way of knowing," or as an appropriate opening move that establishes the "therapeutic alliance," for example. But Kohut would never want empathy to be reduced to this alone. For him empathy was elevated to a vaulted position. He strongly espoused it repeatedly in order to protect it from any effort to redefine or devalue its celebrated role in determining insights, goals, standards, behavior, and the survival of humankind.

Religion as an Indispensable Great Cultural Selfobject

A memorial service for Dr. Kohut was held at the First Unitarian Church in Chicago, where he was a member. Charles Kligerman, a close friend and colleague of Kohut's, stated in that service that during the last two years of his life Kohut held body and soul together by sheer will power alone. With all that was pressing from within and from without at that time, it seems highly significant that Kohut would have spent a portion of his precious final days talking to Robert Randall, a clergyman-psychologist, about religion and self psychology.

Throughout his writings and lectures, Kohut never despised religion. He refused to apply Freud's harshly dismissive evaluation of religion as merely an illusory system with detrimental consequences for humankind. He did, however, strongly reject religious expressions proclaimed to be "facts" of the same order as scientific facts, and he clinically analyzed how archaic narcissistic needs could be expressed in religious forms. His approach to religion expanded, however, just as it did with empathy.

Simply summarized, at first religion was seen as merely an expression of the self, one of the self's unfolding manifestations. Furthermore, he valued religion not only as a creative expression of the self but also as a means for understanding the self—both in its mature and archaic states. Religion, along with other humanities, became a royal road into understanding and appreciating the subjective life of individuals and groups.

Kohut began to posit, however, that religion was not only an expression of the self but something that served to sustain the self. "[A]s a supportive selfobject, religion is not poor by a long shot."[9] Religion and other humanities began to be called "cultural selfobjects."[10] Religion functioned healthily as a kind of large selfobject whose idealization by others helped overcome their dreary and empty lives. Here Kohut expands the place and significance of religion along with its value. Not only is religion to be valued as an expression of the self by which we can learn about the self, it is also to be affirmed as a valued support of the self's own being.

There was one more major expansion of the role and significance of religion. In the following interviews, Kohut no longer speaks in general about cultural selfobjects. He clearly and intentionally identifies three "great" cultural selfobjects and lifts them to prominence. He speaks to Randall about religion as one of these three. Here he not only lifts up the power of religion to sustain selves, but affirms how religion serves in unique and indispensable ways to preserve selves and all humanity. Religion is endorsed, redeemed, and elevated.

Do mental health professionals in general have to accept this about religion in order to utilize the self psychology perspective? No. Do self psychologists have to embrace religion as a legitimate, indispensable source for the healing of selves if they want to be self psychologists? No. Do those who want to feel healthily merged with Kohut and his insights, who want to share the ethos of his perspective, have to embrace religion positively? Probably so. Kohut sent his analytic baby out in the world with the not-so-subtle admonition to embrace the humanities in general and religion in particular as partners in the struggle to make selves whole. This orientation toward religion gives a particular value-cast to self psychology. It is part of the imprint of Kohut's person on the creative movement he started.

Self Psychology as Supraordinate Enterprise

Establishing self psychology as a supraordinate enterprise started early. We have seen how Kohut via the empathic method elevated self psychology to superiority over other ways of psychological knowing, and over the claims of others to possess "psychological data" that was not gleaned through Kohut's method of empathic introspection. As we will see in following chapters, Kohut also asserted supraordinancy of self psychology over Freudian psychology. Here he proclaimed the primacy of narcissistic needs over drive needs, and elevated the developmental primacy of narcissistic needs over drive needs as the bedrock of psychological life.

As time went on, Kohut espoused other ways in which self psychology was the supraordinate enterprise. All other developmental concepts, he suggested, should be subordinated to the developmental insights of self psychology, and all therapeutic approaches should be subordinated in their understanding of themselves, if not in their practice, to the self psychology approach.

But even beyond this, Kohut expanded the role and value of self psychology as an enterprise that was battling for the biological and spiritual survival of humankind.[11] Self psychology is not just a clinical approach for helping individuals with self disorders. Self psychology is engaged in warfare, in the fierce battle for the survival of our present culture and of humanity itself. Indeed, Kohut suggests that self psychology is not only involved in a great battle for human survival, but that self psychology is the *primary hope* by which that survival can happen. Self psychology is subtly proposed as the prescription for "salvation"—individually and culturally.[12]

A cursory introspective assessment regarding Kohut's motivation for this elevation of self psychology could suggest that he was living out fully his nuclear ambitions and ideals. This would be fair to Kohut. But on another level, it is tempting to wonder if Kohut's effort to make self psychology a supraordinate enterprise emerged from internal narcissistic pressures to make sure he left an indelible memorial of his self; an effort to keep his name and creative perspective so vividly alive after his death that he would not suffer a repeat of being forgotten the way he had been as a child. In any case, these elevated roles are value-laden visions in which Kohut has cast self psychology. These are its expanded "reasons for being."

Kohut's analytic baby here takes on warrior and hero dimensions. We authors here have no trouble with the warrior dimension. We support any human endeavor that attempts—with high morals practiced honestly—to battle for the enhancement and endurance of human life. We are, however—perhaps like others who come receptively to the self psychology perspective—more circumspect about the hero dimension. We write this book because we are highly persuaded that Kohut's self psychology perspective can make a hugely deciding difference in how individuals and groups live their lives. We idealize Kohut for this. But we are not his devotees. Kohut's perspective aids greatly in the restoration of humanity, but it is not *the* means by which this can occur. On his best and most cohesive day Kohut would probably concur. Deep in the recesses of his self, however, he may still harbor the vision of self psychology as the Excalibur of hope.

One final observation—or, more accurately, one final hypothesis. There was likely one other somewhat disguised reason Kohut returned to the issue of empathy as a scientific method of observation in his final

address. If Kohut could succeed in getting those in the field of psychology to open themselves to using the empathic-introspective method,
and if he could get them to practice it accurately and consistently, then
he perhaps expected that they, like him, would inevitably see, and become convinced: (a) that self needs are the bedrock of psychological life;
(b) that empathy is the indispensable and ultimate healing power in any
and all therapeutic approaches to healing; and (c) that self psychology
is the default leader in the battle for human survival. Rather than simply
saying, "This is my vision for self psychology; this is how I personally
highly value it and have hopes for its use now and in the future," Kohut
tries to make his case for self psychology's supraordinate status by es-
pousing a scientific method that would presumably lead to that conclusion. While externally it seems he is merely going back in his 1981
address to erase confusion about the empathic-introspective approach,
he is also going back to establish self psychology, via the science of the
empathic method, as the supraordinate psychological viewpoint.

Brief as it is, this is our presentation of Heinz Kohut's self psychology perspective. In the following chapters we will be applying
this perspective as it helps illuminate the reader's own thought, work,
and person.

END NOTES

1.   Kohut, *Self Psychology and the Humanities*, 261.

2.   Kohut, "Introspection, Empathy, and Psychoanalyis."

3.   Kohut, "Introspection, Empathy, and the Semicircle of Mental Health."

4.   Ibid., 544.

5.   Kohut, "Forms and Transformations of Narcissism," 454.

6.   Kohut, *Self Psychology and the Humanities*, 261.

7.   Kohut, *Search for the Self*, 1:451–52; 2:714–15.

8.   Ibid., 2:705.

9.   Kohut, *Self Psychology and the Humanities*, 261.

10.   Ibid., 224–31.

11.   Kohut, *Search for the Self*, 2:516.

12.   Randall, "Soteriological Dimensions in the Work of Heinz Kohut."

2

Self Injury and the Human Condition

Kohut's favorite text on grace is secular—the line from Eugene
O'Neill's *Great God Brown*: "Man is born broken. He lives by
mending. The grace of God is glue."[1]

—Charles Strozier

BEHIND EVERY PSYCHOLOGICAL THEORY is a vision of human fulfillment. An image of optimal health is at work when we name something "neurotic," "sick," or "pathological." We cannot speak of a deficit, a
fault, or a sense of brokenness without an image of human health. Or
as Paul Tillich used to frequently say, every perspective on the human
condition conveys a sense of what is wrong with us, how we can find
healing, and how we can sustain the reality of a new life.

Kohut's theory is certainly no exception. After a long and thorough
immersion in Freudian psychoanalysis, an immersion that earned him
the name "Mr. Psychoanalysis," Kohut emerged with a new perspective
on the human condition. Even while moving away from Freud, Kohut
consistently held a deep reverence and conviction that Freud must *not*
be bypassed. He often charged dissenters with not knowing Freud as
well as they should. Kohut said, "If you always want to lock horns with
Freud, all you do is deprive yourself of his greatness."[2] From the time
that Kohut waved farewell to Freud on a train station platform on June
3, 1938, until his own death in 1981, Kohut ongoingly demonstrated an
abiding respect for Freud's genius. As Charles Strozier puts it, "by the
1950s one could say there were those who knew the master as well as
Kohut but no one knew the master better.... He never stopped quoting
and writing about Freud."[3] In fact, for as long as possible, Kohut tried to
couch his newly emerging perspective in traditional Freudian language.

Gradually, however, a new vision of human life burst forth. This vision was less pessimistic and less conflict-driven than Freud's darker portrait of humanity.

From about the mid-1960s until his death in 1981, Kohut began to distance himself from traditional psychoanalytic reading and thinking in order to creatively explore his own ideas. Rather than being an authority on what other analysts were saying, Kohut allowed his own creativity to flourish. While it was certainly not unusual to see non-analytic individuals move away from drive theory, it was indeed unusual to see a man who had been so utterly committed to traditional psychoanalysis turn away from it. In the 1950s and 60s, drive theory practically defined psychoanalysis, especially in the United States. While some ego psychologists such as Erik Erikson wanted to include social and cultural factors in looking at psychological dynamics, they did not give up on drive theory. Those non-drive theorists outside of psychoanalytic circles were simply dismissed as not truly understanding psychoanalytic theory. But no one could say that of Kohut. His ability to teach traditional Freudian theory was renowned.

Thus, to see Kohut and self psychology as merely offering new therapeutic techniques for psychological health is to miss the fundamental change in framework his theory offered. In short, he provides a new paradigm of human possibilities. In an earlier era, Kohut's departure from Freud would have experienced the same fate of Adler, Jung, Horney, and others. Put simply, he would have been banned from the psychoanalytic club. Yet while Kohut's ideas raised the eyebrows of many traditional analysts, he was still generally perceived as part of the psychoanalytic community and taught at various institutes. Traditional drive theorists may argue that Kohut has rejected the backbone of psychoanalytic theory, but his work has not been rejected in the same way that previous non-drive theorists were dismissed. Perhaps Kohut was not excommunicated from psychoanalytic circles, in part, because he explained human drives from the vantage point of another paradigm. He did not deny human destructiveness and out-of-control sexuality. He simply accounted for them on the basis of an alternative theory.

DRIVES ARE NOT THE PRIMARY PROBLEM

Even within psychoanalytic circles, Kohut was not the first psychoanalyst to move away from Freud's famous drive theory. But the differences between a drive and deficit model became *decisively clear* in Kohut's writings. The break from drive theory was accompanied by an alternative framework for understanding why the drives become problematic. Inherent, destructive drives were not the true enemy. Instead, they revealed a deeper issue that had already taken place, namely injuries to the self that left it weak. These self injuries resulted from earlier deprivations. The picture of humanity in a constant state of internal conflict faded away. Mental health was no longer conceived as mastering, taming, and controlling these rather beastly drives that sought direct release. For Kohut, the whole language of drive theory did not capture the deeper experience of self injury. Again, Kohut did not merely critique drive theory. Instead, he explained drive theory in terms of an alternative interpretation of the human condition. He attempted to demonstrate how the "drives" could be better understood as an outgrowth of earlier, pre-Oedipal injuries. He went beyond attacking the Freudian model; he incorporated it within an alternative framework. He did not deny the *experience* of being driven. But he placed this experience into a perspective that denied that the drives represent the rock-bottom, pivotal issue behind all human problems. The drives are a problem because of something deeper; they do not represent the central dilemma. They are an outgrowth of a more pervasive issue: early self injuries.

Again, for many, this move away from drive theory seemed like a move away from psychoanalysis itself. In other words, traditional psychoanalytic theory seemed utterly steeped in the conviction that human motivation is rooted in the biological sphere. Drives seek direct expression and are frequently destructive in nature. They must be rechanneled or sublimated into socially acceptable behavior. Instinctual, pleasure-seeking impulses inevitably run antagonistically into the necessary rules of social life. An unending war between drives and society can be managed but never eliminated. The conflict is ever-present. Instincts and social prohibitions will remain bitter enemies till the very end.

This Freudian picture of the psyche is rather unflattering, but Freud insisted that it was realistic. In fact, Freud frequently remarked that his theory of the drives provided the third major blow to humanity's inflated picture of itself. The first blow was Copernicus's realization that the earth is not the center of the heavens; the second was Darwin's discovery of our connection with the rest of animal life; and the third was Freud's sobering realization of the sexual lust and aggressive impulses that motivate our so-called "decent" behavior. Over the course of Freud's life, he became more and more convinced that the beast within us all needs to be tamed. The very possibility of civilization depends on this taming. Life itself carries within it an impulse toward death and destruction. This struggle is within us from our first breath until our last. Any view of human innocence must swallow this bitter pill. We are innately, inherently, and biologically destructive. We will never eradicate this inclination; instead, we must learn to live with it. While the earlier Freud had clearly understood the power of our sexual instincts, the later Freud also grasped the power of our aggressive instincts as well. Indeed, even the cultured gentleman is a tamed savage.

> Early on Freud committed himself to an instinct theory. The crucial assumption of that theory, grounded in nineteenth-century psychology, is that it takes psychic energies, or cathexes, to run the self. Without this energy, so went the logic of the metaphor, the operations of the "psychic apparatus" made no sense. Without drives there appeared to be no explanation for motivation.[4]

In contrast to this Freudian conception of innate destructiveness, Kohut insisted that our original drives are *not* inherently destructive. They are made destructive by early narcissistic injury. Freud, for Kohut, had confused the wounded self with the natural self. As he put it:

> The baby cries, and the baby cries angrily when whatever needs to be done is not done immediately. But there is no original need to destroy; the original need is to establish an equilibrium. . . . Speaking in biological terms, we will, of course, acknowledge the presence of a preformed apparatus (teeth and nails and muscles) that determines the specific patterns in which the continuum assertiveness-aggression-destructiveness manifest itself. But, psychoanalytically speaking, the human baby is not comparable to a beast of prey.[5]

Again, in the midst of this pessimistic Freudian depiction of the human condition, Kohut dared to assert that what Freud had called *primary* drives were in fact *secondary* problems. It was with fear and trembling that a person might suggest that Freud, the very pioneer of "depth" psychology, did not see deeply enough. But in a sense, this is what Kohut suggested. In discussing those who are fixated on drive gratification, Kohut makes the following statement:

When we analyze adults who suffer from narcissistic disturbances—individuals who make incessant demands for gratification, we may get the impression that they were spoiled as children. We reason: there was continuous drive-gratification, so those people became fixated on their drives and that is why they became sick. But that's not so. They didn't become fixated on the drive because they were spoiled, because of drive-gratification. They became fixated on drives because their budding selves were overlooked, were not responded to. They turned to drive-gratification (and later remained fixed on it) because they tried to relieve their depression—they tried to escape the horrible feeling that nobody was responding to them. Such people may have had mothers who satisfied their drives continuously, yet failed to respond with pride and pleasure to the child's independent self.[6]

Again, drives *become* problematic because of earlier psychological injuries to the self. Excessive drives are an attempt at self-repair. We fixate on them and attempt to repair our self injuries *through* them. It is not "natural" to be violently aggressive, sexually intoxicated, constantly hungry, or insatiable. When this insatiability emerges, it *does so* in an attempt to fill a void, heal a deficit, or repair damage that has already occurred. *Human brokenness precedes human destructiveness*. The issue is not so much "taming" wild desires as healing and repairing injuries to the self. Destructive inclinations emerge from the experience of self fragmentation, or what is often called "disintegration anxiety." It is when the self is shaky or feels that it is "coming undone" that it expresses its most destructive tendencies. Feeling wounded and overwhelmed with vulnerability, we attempt to reverse this sense of coming undone. We "hold ourselves together" through dramatic expressions of rage, sexuality, and a host of addictive behaviors. These fixations seem to supply the self with a temporary glue which binds it. These obsessions compensate for feelings of disintegration. They hide our vulnerability. When we are raging, for instance, we feel strong rather than vulnerable, weak, and shaky. Thus, the irony is that when we appear the most destructive, we may actually be feeling the most threatened.

It is important to note here that Kohut is *not* denying the very real nature of human destructiveness. He is not ignoring the obvious violence all around us. He is simply saying that this destructiveness is not rooted in our biology. It is not a natural, innate, essential outgrowth of being human. We are not "hardwired" toward destructiveness. We do not have to spend a lifetime struggling to "tame" what is inherent within us. Instead, we need to search beneath the ugliness of destructive behavior to find its source. While competitiveness and healthy aggression are natural, destructive aggression is always a *byproduct of self injury*. Rage is intricately related to narcissistic injury. Destructive anger results not from our biology but from non-empathic environments that have fostered injured selves. Rages may indeed be overreactions. But they are attempts to repair self fractures. To repeat, they are based more on wounds than on drives. Hostility results from a fear of humiliation. When self-esteem is threatened, destructiveness is an unfortunate attempt to restore the self. Narcissistic rage is based on an urge for revenge, an attempt to undo the offense of another, an effort to regain control. As Volney Gay puts it, "From a moralistic point of view, the patient's rage is wrong and unjustified. From an empathic, analytic point of view these rageful responses, like fragmentation experiences, must be understood as signs of the patient's profound narcissistic suffering."[7]

Normal, healthy aggression can be used in the service of obtaining our goals and fulfilling our ambitions. As Kohut puts it, "The drive component, or the drive source, the psychobiological readiness toward aggression, can be requisitioned, as it were, in the service of object-libidinal strivings and in overcoming obstacles of independently experienced competitors or other resistances."[8] Healthy assertiveness emerges from a cohesive self; destructive anger emerges from a fragmented self. Kohut puts this directly:

> ... no purely destructive urge arises so long as the environment is reasonably responsive and empathic. . . . When the environment becomes traumatically unresponsive, then the original, broader psychological configurations disintegrate and you may indeed see isolated rage, the isolated, indiscriminate wish to destroy, to kill, to tear apart because no empathic response is forthcoming. In other words, if empathy failures of the self-object environment are within nontraumatizing limits—optimal frustration of the child's need for empathic responses—then there are minor swings in the psychic equilibrium of the child, manifested by an increase of the child's aggressive assertiveness and healthy demandingness. If, on the other hand, the empathy failures are of a traumatic degree, then the complex psychological constellations break up, fragment, and behavioral manifestations appear that

can be referred to as motivated by an aggressive drive. The drive, then, is not a primary *psychological* given.[9]

Kohut goes on to suggest that the perspective one takes toward these basic drives will enormously influence and color the therapeutic approach one takes with individuals. If a raw destructiveness is believed to be a basic part of the human constitution, one will approach the patient far differently than if one sees this destructiveness as a byproduct of self injury. One's philosophy of human nature determines the actual clinical practice in which one is engaged. For Kohut, there is a struggle with helplessness beneath rage, a deep deficit beneath destructive anger, an experience of empathic failure underlying our hatred.

DRIVES AND ORIGINAL SIN: FROM AUGUSTINE TO FREUD

Long before any psychological thinker begins to theorize about human nature, he or she has already been influenced by theories concerning the human condition. We each inherit a world of conceptual assumptions, implicit images, and metaphors concerning human nature.[10] Psychological thinking may distance itself from the philosophical assumptions in which it grows up, but these assumptions nevertheless form the matrix out of which we begin to officially think about ourselves.

It is helpful to place Freud's drive theory within a larger framework of intellectual history, which emphasizes humanity's innate capacity for destructiveness, violence, and evil. This negative view of inherent human evil has deeply influenced the manner in which individuals have approached each other. Put simply, it suggests that human nature cannot be trusted. This dark portrait of the human condition in the Western intellectual tradition has been hugely influenced by the towering figure of St. Augustine. Though previous thinkers clearly talked about inherited impulses, Augustine is often celebrated or attacked as the primary architect of the doctrine of original sin. This view of the human condition has been a very gloomy one. It has insisted that while humanity was originally created in a pure and innocent state, that innocence has been lost because of the sin of the first couple. Augustine, and most of pre-Enlightenment thought, took the Genesis story as a literal, historical account of humanity's beginnings and first struggle with evil.

It is commonly, but mistakenly, believed that Augustine proclaimed sin to be rooted in the rebellious behavior of Adam and Eve. But this was not what Augustine actually taught. Augustine was too astute an observer of the human condition to believe that it was rebelliousness itself that created the problem. Instead, it was the psychological dynamics and *thinking process* that preceded this act. In other words, it was the growing conviction of the first humans that they were the source of their own lives and hence could replace God. It was the emergence of this unwarranted self-sufficiency, this arrogance, which prompted the first disobedience. Put in psychological terms, Augustine was not simply a behaviorist. He was interested in the underlying dynamics and thought process that led to the act of eating the forbidden fruit. As Augustine put it, "This then, is the original evil: man regards himself as his own light, and turns away from that light which would make himself a light if he would set his heart on it. This evil came first in secret and the result was the other evil, which was committed in the open."[11]

Augustine argued that while Adam and Eve had been created pure, innocent, and even perfect, their sinful pride and rebellion had placed them in antagonism with God, and consequently, they were banished from the Garden of Eden. Because they had been created perfect, their sin was even more outrageous. Augustine puts it this way:

> The injunction forbidding the eating of one kind of food, where such an abundant supply of other foods was available, was so easy to observe, so brief to remember; above all, it was given at a time when desire was not yet in opposition to the will. That opposition came later as a result of the punishment of the transgression. Therefore the unrighteousness of violating the prohibition was so much the greater, in proportion to the ease with which it could have been observed and fulfilled.[12]

Thus, for Augustine, the first sin was completely inexcusable. In Adam's pre-fallen state, his desires were not yet unruly, so he was not impulsively overwhelmed. Instead, for Augustine, this first act of rebellion grew out of Adam's pride. Adam wanted to usurp God and make himself the center of the universe. Thus, through this historical first couple, sin entered human history. Originally created to follow the calm voice of reason, their natures were not spoiled and contaminated by sin. They were not *inclined* to act in sinful and destructive ways. For Augustine, even sexuality, which was experienced in the Garden as calm, loving, and non-passionate, was now full of passion, lust, and irrational desire.

Humanity's nature had been tainted. But what is more, the first couple's offspring—the whole human race—had been perversely affected.

Augustine particularly forced this point against an opposing group allied around Pelagius, another important figure in early Christian thought. Pelagius had argued that we are *not* born in a state of sin. Instead, we have the capacities to please God and keep the commandments. Adam and Eve may have set a very bad example, but we did not inherit their guilt. For Pelagius, we each have the capacity to choose the way of goodness and truth over sin. But Augustine rigorously attacked the Pelagians for spreading this heresy that we are born in a state of goodness and only later "fall." For Augustine, because each human being bears Adam's guilt, we are hardly born innocent. We deserve damnation. Hence, Augustine frequently argued against the Pelagians that unbaptized infants, should they die, would be damned to hell.

Augustine believed that our fallen state has pushed our drives out of control. This condition is called "concupiscence," an inordinate state of desire in which we are full of excessive longing and lust. We naturally crave things that cannot possibly deliver what we expect from them. We attempt to turn limited and finite objects into our source of happiness and meaning; hence, we over-desire them. Again, these desires are distorted because of sin. The idea of "created innocence" applied only to the original couple. Everyone else in the history of the world has been born with unruly, destructive impulses. Our desires and drives are excessive and dangerous.

Some may quickly argue that Augustine actually came to humanity's defense in arguing against the Manicheans, who taught that the entire world was created evil. For the Manicheans, physical existence was *created* corrupt, and hence, an inferior god was responsible for human life. But if human existence was created corrupt, reasoned Augustine, then human beings cannot possibly be held responsible for their own behavior. Put simply, if we were "made" evil, we can hardly be held responsible. Augustine insisted that God was not responsible for our sin. While we were originally created good, that goodness has been lost through the freedom of the first human pair. Thus, Augustine's anti-Manichaean battle attempts to explain how a good creation went wrong. While the original creation was good, humanity corrupted itself through prideful disobedience. This, while Adam and Eve may have experienced a temporary period of innocence, the practical, existential implication for the rest of us is that we *are* born with evil inclinations. We are guilty for simply existing, inherently flawed and corrupt.

Many have been quite critical of this Augustinian doctrine of original sin. It is blamed for leading to an exaggerated sense of self-disgust, as well as a profound distrust in our own feelings, thoughts, perceptions, and "reality." With a profound sense of our own corruption, critics argue, we are often set up for being controlled by others. We are, after all, fundamentally flawed and defective, so why should we trust our own judgments about anything? Put simply, the notion of original sin is accused of being an abusive doctrine. Paul Ricoeur puts it sharply:

> The harm that has been done to souls, during the centuries of Christianity, first by literal interpretation of the story of Adam, and then by the confusion of this myth, treated as history, with later speculations, principally Augustinian, about original sin, will never be adequately told. In asking the faithful to confess belief in this mythico-speculative mass and to accept it as a self-sufficient explanation, the theologians have unduly required a *sacrificium intellectus* where what was needed was to awaken believers to a symbolic superintelligence of their actual condition.[13]

For Augustine's critics, to state that the very minute we come into this world we are already damned, sinners before we draw our first breath, is indeed a shaming and dehumanizing doctrine. It contributes to feelings of worthlessness and disgust. To say that we are each born *already guilty* is to blame the victim. As Alan Watts puts it:

> To begin at the beginning of the trouble, it is utterly incomprehensible that one man's disobedience should have involved the entire race in the guilt for his sin, and, what is more, made them liable to everlasting damnation. This seems in flat opposition to all our ideas of personal responsibility and integrity, the more so when there is not explanation of the channels whereby the taint of original sin passes from generation to generation.[14]

Further, a causal explanation may have seemed satisfactory as long as we could point toward a historical Adam and a pre-fallen state of perfection. Contemporary evolutionary science, however, has rendered such a "Golden Era" in human history impossible. A literal, historical, space-and-time fall contradicts humanity's evolutionary history. Also, death was a part of life long before humanity started making decisions, and contrary to many previous theologians, nature did not become brutal and competitive because of Adam's choice. Instead, a struggle for survival was a central aspect of evolutionary history long before humanity arrived on the scene.

Many theologians have suggested that rather than offering a historical explanation, the story of Adam and Eve is a symbolic representation of human experience, i.e., that we all somehow mishandle our freedom in the face of anxiety and act in destructive ways. Further, we each *do indeed* inherit a world of distorted values, alienation, and deception. None of us makes our first unhealthy choice uninfluenced by the problems of the past. Thus, while we may no longer believe that we are mysteriously linked to Adam's choice, we can recognize that Adam's story is our story as well. *The language of inheritance, in this sense, can help us recognize that an atmosphere of destructiveness precedes human choice and is much larger than our own autonomous decisions.* Thus, we might state it this way: Augustine's brilliant, but exaggerated, explanation of original sin—which attempted to salvage human goodness from the Gnostic idea that created existence is evil—was sabotaged by his development of original guilt. For it is very difficult to see how any individual person can be held responsible for a biologically inherited condition.

Perhaps another exaggerated element in the Augustinian teaching about original sin is the catastrophic manner in which God reacted to the first sin. If we think in literal terms (as Augustine did), getting banished from the Garden, being sentenced to death, condemned to the vicious pains of childbirth, and, for most of humanity, being eternally damned, seems like a harsh overreaction. If we even begin to employ any sort of parental analogy to this scene, we would be aghast at such a harsh, even cruel, parental reaction. This is very serious punishment for a single act of disobedience. *In Kohutian language,* this would seem to point toward God's own narcissistic rage and temper tantrum over our failure to mirror the Divine image and offer the kind of adoration to which God's fragile sense of self felt entitled. Again, if the parental designation of "Father" or "Mother" is applied to our image of the Divine, the prospect of eternal damnation for the unwise self-assertion of a child seems rather extreme. Put more directly, what loving parent would possibly create a place of eternal darkness for a child who didn't respond favorably to the parent's highly conditional love? Where is the ongoing source of nurture, care, and love in this picture? Some may quickly add that God does not wish the damnation of anyone. But who set up this system in the first place? Who made eternal damnation the consequence of disobedience? Would not other, more compassionate "learning lessons" be appropriate here?

Perhaps it is because we don't *think though* the logical consequences of some of these images of God that we are able to work with people, enjoy their company, donate to charities with them, and even respect their ethical convictions and character while simultaneously believing that apart from a dramatic conversion to Christianity, they will agonizingly squirm, scream, and beg for help in eternal flames. *From a Kohutian perspective, the concept of hell seems more like narcissistic revenge than love.* It is the ultimate punishment—the one from which there is no rehabilitation. As Leslie Weatherhead wrote in *The Christian Agnostic*, this is why the idea of eternal damnation is so offensively pointless: the punishment goes on and on with no hope for rehabilitation or change.[15] Eternal damnation involves no point of intervention in which a voice says, "Stop. This is enough." Instead, the punishment simply endures forever and ever. An unknown source quoted by Weatherhead beautifully calls into question this whole notion of eternal damnation:

> A man who was entirely careless of spiritual things died and went to Hell. And he was much missed on earth by his old friends. His business manager went down to the gates of Hell to see if there were any chance of bringing him back. But, though he pleaded for the gates to be opened, the iron bars never yielded. His cricket captain went also and besought Satan to let him out just for the remainder of the season. But there was no response. His minister went also and argued, saying, "He was not altogether bad. Let him have another chance. Let him out just this once." Many other friends of his went also and pleaded with Satan saying, "Let him out. Let him out." But when his mother came, she spoke no word of his release. Quietly, and with a strange catch in her voice, she said to Satan, "*Let me in.*" For love goes down through the gates of Hell and there redeems the damned.[16]

Surely, psychotherapy has helped us understand more directly the importance of the kind of empathic, healing care revealed in this story. In fact, Tillich suggests that psychotherapy aids us in seeing the more maternal aspect of our image of God.

> One can say that psychotherapy has replaced the emphasis on the demanding yet remote God by an emphasis on his self-giving nearness. It is the modification of the image of the threatening

father—which was so important in Freud's attack on religion—by elements of the image of the embracing and supporting mother. If I were permitted to express a bold suggestion, I would say that psychotherapy and the experiences of pastoral counseling have helped to reintroduce the female element, so conspicuously lacking in most Protestantism, into the idea of God.[17]

While God may not be perceived as a Cosmic Enabler who shields us from all consequences of our destructive behavior, a grace-filled image of God moves us away from the harsh and even abusive image of eternal punishment.

The connection between this longstanding Western religious view of original sin and Freud's dark vision is obvious. For both Augustine and Freud, our drives are inherently destructive, innately out of control, and biologically problematic. Again, this is the condition in which we are born. *We don't simply enter a world of human destructiveness; instead, we have destructive tendencies when we show up!* Life has been, and always will be, riddled with the conflict between our basic drives and those things we must do to protect civilization. Augustine envisioned a cosmos in which an eternal split will separate the damned from God and the elect. Similarly, Freud envisioned a world in which a basic conflict between *eros* and *thanatos*, or the life and death instincts, will *always* be present. For neither thinker is there an ultimate or final reconciliation. Unlike the earlier Christian theologian, Origen, who had discussed a final restoration of unity in the cosmos in which evil would be redeemed, Augustine sees an eternal split between the saved and the damned. The warfare continues and never ceases. Similarly, Freud views conflict as part of the very essence of existence.

FROM "GUILTY MAN" TO "TRAGIC MAN"

Kohut's shift from a drive orientation to a deficit orientation is captured in his designations of "Guilty Man" and "Tragic Man." "Guilty Man" refers to the classic Freudian portrait of the human condition, an image dominated by the experience of guilt over drives that are inherently excessive. As we have seen, this image sees humanity in a constant battle to tame its own nature as it tries to restrain the natural beast within. Our biological drives are dangerous. We must approach them with caution and a deep concern for their destructive potential. Hence, our primary experience is one of guilt.

In fact, Freud eventually came to the position that the innate aggressive instinct within human beings threatens the very fabric of civilization. As he put it, "I adopt the standpoint, therefore, that the inclination to aggressiveness is an original, self-subsisting instinctual disposition in man, and I return to my view that it constitutes the greatest impediment to civilization."[18] Aggression and violence, for the seasoned Freud, are natural. While social and political factors may influence the destructive powers within us, the fact remains that an innate destructiveness threatens human life every step of the way.

Paul Tillich held a deep respect for Freud's sober estimation of the human condition. He applauded Freud's insight that conscious reason does not rule the day, but is instead often in the grip of unconscious and irrational tendencies. Yet Tillich insisted that Freud's brilliant analysis confused our existential predicament with our "essence" or created nature. In other words, Freud provided a brilliant portrait of estranged existence but he does not tell us about our essential being. Tillich puts it this way:

> His dismay of culture shows that he is very consistent in his negative judgments about man as existentially distorted. Now if you see man only from the point of view of existence and not from the point of view of essence, only from the point of estrangement and not from the view of essential goodness, then this consequence is unavoidable. And it is true of Freud in this respect.[19]

For Tillich, estrangement is universal but it does not indicate that our essential or original natures are corrupt. There is nothing within our basic nature which demands that we act in destructive or unhealthy ways. Stated differently, our problem is not our biology. Thus, while Tillich understood Freud's description of estranged existence as a "gift"[20] to Christian theology, he nevertheless believed that Freud located that estrangement in the wrong place, namely our constitutional tendencies. Indeed, this is precisely the charge Tillich would make against the literalized view of inherited sin in Augustine's biological transmission theory.

Tillich's colleague at Union Theological Seminary in New York, Reinhold Niebuhr, also deeply valued Freud's insights but believed that Freud locates our excessive desires and destructive inclinations in the wrong place—our biological disposition.[21] Destructive tendencies do not automatically occur as a result of our biological makeup. Put theologically, we are not hardwired to sin. If we were, we could not possibly be held responsible. Violent aggression and unruly sexuality do not arise from our basic nature.

In contrast to this drive-oriented, guilty image of the human condition, Kohut set forth the position that our "fragmented drivenness" emerges from an injured or wounded self. Rather than a state of ongoing guilt over unruly drives, our condition is tragic in that we seek to fulfill, with difficulty, the program of our nuclear, but damaged, self. Our most basic problem is not our biological drives; instead, our greatest struggle is with our narcissistic vulnerability. "Tragic Man" is more concerned with achieving ideals than with simply seeking pleasure. But why does Kohut call this "tragic?" Because this striving to realize one's true potential is frustrated by the empathic failures in the child's early experience.

It is possible, with a creative stretch, to understand the traditional concept of the fall from a Kohutian perspective. The original state of the child is one of undisturbed narcissism. The child has the capacity for healthy development in an empathic, responsive, psychologically supportive environment. In this early experience is a kind of hope that life will perpetually provide perfect responses. This is an empathic "Garden of Eden," a world of perfect psychological responsiveness. This is a world *before* woundedness, an existence *prior to* narcissistic injury. Yet this world inevitably bumps into the narcissistic vulnerability of limited environmental support. The emotional conditions necessary for this process of self development are invariably lacking. This is a kind of "fall" from a state of innocence and possibility. The original possibility for harmony has been lost. One is banned from the world of undisturbed equilibrium and placed into a jungle of narcissistic vulnerability where psychological threats are ever-present. Lynn Greenlee elaborates on how this Kohutian vision can be paralleled with the symbolic Genesis account of the fall.

> The Fall of Adam and Eve in the Garden involves the basic elements of the human condition that Kohut has astutely observed in the narcissistic line of development. Originally in perfect harmony (undisturbed narcissistic equilibrium), Adam and Eve, in the omnipotent act of attempting to "be like God," fell, and for the first time experienced narcissistic vulnerability and its byproduct, shame. The infant's experience of failure to receive optimal mirroring of omnipotent strivings leads to narcissistic vulnerability, "a ubiquitous burden of man, a part of the human condition from which no one is exempt . . ." (Kohut, 1977, p. 292). It is true that Adam and Eve experienced guilt at the Fall (Narramore, 1984),

but the primary experience was one of shame. Shame reflects feelings of inadequacy, defect, and failure leading to withdrawal and concealment. Guilt, on the other hand, is a feeling related to the transgression of a wrong that leads toward confession, self-revelation, and the goal of forgiveness (Morrison, 1984). With the realization of their nakedness, Adam and Eve covered themselves, then hid from God. It was at this point of a heightened sense of their narcissistic vulnerability that they experienced shame and a fragmentation of the self as they were cut off from the perfect selfobject: God. There was a breech of the empathic connection between God and humanity in terms of having a self-object that maintains the narcissistic equilibrium fully and perfectly that is relived in every child in the struggle to fulfill the pattern of the nuclear self (the *imago Dei*) in the face of the empathic failures of human self-objects. Kohut's emphasis on the transmission of self pathology from parents with narcissistic defects to their children highlights the generational transmissions of the "sins of the fathers" (Exodus 34:7).[22]

It is important to note that even though Kohut is less pessimistic than Freud about the human condition, *he nevertheless believes that a fall into woundedness is inevitable and universal.* No one completely escapes narcissistic injury. As Jule Miller III put it, "no one gets through childhood without some experience of being the outcast from Eden."[23]

In previous publications, one of the authors of this book has argued that Kohut's perspective on the human condition can perhaps be better placed within the framework of Ireneaus's theological anthropology, over against that of Augustine.[24] Ireneaus, perhaps the most significant second-century theologian, argued for a far less catastrophic "fall" than Augustine's later work. Ireneaus set forth an image of humanity as more weak and insecure than depraved. Human beings were *not* created perfect as Augustine would later argue. They were in fact created immature and in need of spiritual progress. Through a process of trial and error, humanity could grow and develop in its likeness of God. We may be created in God's "image" (bodily powers, reason, and choice) but we have to grow into God's "likeness," which refers to a cultivated sense of God's character. This is a process of gradual growth. As Irenaeus put it:

> A mother, for example, can provide perfect food for a child, but at that point he cannot digest food which is suitable for someone older. Similarly, God himself certainly could have provided hu-

manity with perfection from the beginning. Humanity, however, was immature and unable to lay hold of it.[25]

As a created being, Adam could not be perfect because, as Ireneaus insisted, only uncreated reality is perfect. Adam could not have handled perfection. Instead, God allowed Adam to grow into a more mature person with a stronger commitment to goodness. For Ireneaus, the "fall" of Adam does not have the disastrous nature and evil consequences that it later had for Augustine. Adam was immature, was tempted, and fell. His discriminatory powers were not very developed. In this sense, Ireneaus offers a more compassionate and even empathic view of humanity's ills. In a sense, the fall into sin was a part of growing up and learning about life. The experience of sin helps us appreciate God's kindness.

Put simply, this is a non-shaming view of the fall. Getting kicked out of the Garden was part of our development toward a higher level of existence. Suffering is not the horrible consequence of Adam's sin; instead, it is a means of spiritual development. By concretely experiencing the differences between sin and virtue, we can gradually prefer goodness. And this gradual process will require patience. For Ireneaus, we want too much too fast.

> People who do not wait for the period of growth, who attribute the weakness of their nature to God, are completely unreasonable. They understand neither God nor themselves; they are ungrateful and never satisfied. At the outset they refuse to be what they were made: human beings who are subject to passions. They override the law of human nature; they already want to be like God the Creator before they even become human beings. They want to do away with all the differences between the uncreated God and created humans.[26]

Ireneaus believes we should attempt to be fully human before we try to imitate God. Further, our suffering and pain are *not* the punishments for a dreadful fall in our past. Instead of incurring the wrath of God and its radical disconnection from our being, we instead have an opportunity to glimpse better the compassionate help of a God with whom we are still connected.

The question of how much human life is estranged from its Source, of how fallen is our basic nature, has plagued Christian thought throughout its history. Suffice it to say that, in general, those who have followed the Augustinian tradition have emphasized a break or radical discontinuity between humanity and God. Those who have been more inclined toward Irenaeus's view do not believe that the fall has led to such a dramatic break between God and humanity. An Augustinian view often argues that human nature is so utterly inept in seeking a spiritual path that God's grace is necessary for us to even seek God. Others believe that our natures have not been so damaged that we do not have the capacity and the propensity to seek God. The later, more optimistic view of the human condition seems far more capable of housing the views of the non-drive-oriented perspective of Kohut. For Irenaeus, sin is associated with immaturity, insecurity, and ignorance. Our suffering, rather than resulting from the wrath of God, is part of psychologically growing up.

For both Kohut and traditional Christian theology, what we have called "sin" has to do with "missing the mark" of our authentic personhood. Kohut understands mental health as functioning in accordance to our true design or our essential nature. The tragedy of life is to not fulfill our nuclear self-goals. While Kohut does not seem to go as far as Jung in arguing for an innate, essential blueprint that precedes human experience (the idea that we are already born whole with a mission built into our very genes), he does believe that the earliest psychological experiences nudge us in the direction of a "nuclear" self with its potentials for fulfillment. The goal of therapy is always firming up the self and helping patients fulfill their nuclear self-ambitions. These ambitions will not be the grandiose, narcissistic hopes of childhood. But they will be a transformed grandiosity that faces our own limitations without losing the enthusiasm of our goals and fulfillment.

It is worth noting Charles Kligerman's words at Heinz Kohut's memorial: "Heinz was ready for his death. He always had a firm conviction that each person had almost an inborn agenda, a destiny to fulfill, that compared to eternity it mattered little how long one lived provided one lived up to one's potentialities in pursuing his ideal."[27] Early in life, a "design" for our lives emerges and it is crucial that we fulfill it. A central program for our life, even a sense of "calling," seems to be present. In a sense, this is Kohut's rendition of the *imago Dei*, or the image of the Divine, within each person. It is an invitation to achieve, even in the midst of the struggles of human life, the basic ambitions and goals of the self.

Crayton Rowe and David MacIsaac remind us that while Kohut does not provide an explicit, concrete picture of the healthy personality, he nevertheless offers a psychological portrait that involves some of the following characteristics: (a) a capacity for empathic attunement to others, (b) a curiosity and wish to understand the needs of others, (c) an ability to compromise and delay one's needs for the sake of the other, (d) an ability to love, (e) the capacity to be creative, (f) a sense of humor, and (g) enthusiasm for one's life.[28] It is particularly important to note the characteristic of being able, from time to time, to sacrifice one's own needs for the sake of others. While self-sacrifice should not become a permanent way of life in our relationships, it is important to include the needs of others in our view of human fulfillment. One must coordinate with the needs of others. There is always a dance—sometimes a difficult one—of coordinating our own needs with those around us. As Don Browning's work regularly reminds us, this struggle to coordinate our own needs for "actualization" with the actualization of others is not always noticed and adequately recognized in humanistic psychologies of self-actualization.[29]

Also, a secure sense of self is intricately tied up with the ability to love and care for others. As Kohut puts it, "the more secure a person is regarding his own acceptability, the more certain his sense of who he is, and the more safely internalized his system of values—the more self-confidently and effectively will he be able to offer his love . . . without undue fear of rejection and humiliation."[30] The ability to love depends upon having a relatively stable and secure sense of self. And this ability to have a secure sense of self is a gift from those important caretakers in our lives. Indeed, we love because we have first *been* loved. Grace precedes our ability to love and care for others.

MOVING AWAY FROM THE OEDIPUS CONFLICT

If anything is clear in Freudian psychology, it is that the Oedipus story is the very centerpiece of the human dilemma. This story reveals both the sexual and aggressive drives as it expresses the drama of the psyche's fundamental conflict. Freud introduced the concept of the Oedipus complex as early as 1900:

> Being in love with the one parent and hating the other are among the essential constituents of the stock of psychical impulses which is formed [in childhood] and which [in children destined to grow up neurotic] is of such importance in determining their symptoms. This discovery is confirmed by a legend that has come

down to us from classical antiquity: a legend whose profound and
universal power to move can only be understood if the hypothesis
I have put forward in regard to the psychology of children has an
equally universal validity. What I have in mind is the legend of
King Oedipus and Sophocles' drama which bears his name.[31]

This famous story, for Freud, reveals the story of all of us. The fact that
Oedipus unwittingly killed his father and ended up marrying his own
mother points toward a deep, unconscious wish buried in the human
psyche. For Freud, all humans go through a desire for connection with
the parent of the opposite sex, as well as angry and jealous feelings toward the same-sex parent. The underlying urge is to get rid of the parent
of the same sex so that one can possess the object of one's desires. For
boys, a sexual attraction for the mother comes equipped with a fear of
retaliation by the father. Our mental health depends greatly on our ability to resolve these particular issues.

For many traditional psychoanalysts, denying the centrality and significance of this Oedipus complex was tantamount to heresy. Yet Kohut
interpreted it as an outgrowth of a previous problem. The Oedipus complex, in a sense, was symptomatic of an earlier and deeper issue within
the child's psyche. The Oedipus *period*, for Kohut, does not represent a
universal and inevitable conflict that works out the innate drives of sex
and aggression. Instead, this period of life, when problematic, expresses
pre-Oedipal injuries to the self. As Kohut scholar Marcia Dobson suggests, Oedipus lived comfortably in Corinth *until* he received an insult
from a drunken man at a party. Oedipus was accused of being a bastard.[32] It was *after* these injurious words (which created self-doubt) that
he went to an oracle and raised the question, "Who am I?" The oracle
then tells Oedipus that he will end up killing his father and marrying his
mother. Oedipus flees to Thebes to escape this fate. On the way he is run
off the road by an older man (who happens to be his father). He retaliates
and kills the man. He then enters Thebes where he guesses the riddle of
the Sphinx, and thereby becomes the king. He marries the queen, who is
actually his mother. Oedipus then realizes that he has tragically fulfilled
the oracle's prediction.

A Kohutian interpretation of this famous story points out that the
first event in the tale, the drunkard's comment about Oedipus being a
bastard, involved an injury to Oedipus's sense of self. After this insult,
Oedipus fell into shame and self-doubt. The injury was in fact signifi-

cant enough that Oedipus made a long journey to visit the Delphic oracle. This comment pushed Oedipus into a search for his true identity, a search that revealed a very fragile and shaky self. Put in Kohutian language, Oedipus was motivated more by disintegrating anxiety than by castration anxiety.[33] The pre-Oedipal self injuries, then, are more pervasive and significant than the Oedipus complex itself. In fact, the Oedipus "complex" can be handled quite calmly and successfully if a supportive, empathic psychological environment has already been set up. Again, this position sounded radical to the traditional psychoanalytic community. The Oedipus complex was a non-negotiable item of belief, a part of the official creed. Not only did Kohut minimize its significance as the centerpiece of human struggle, he explained it as an outgrowth of a deeper and more pervasive struggle. Hence, he did not simply attack an existing theory. Instead, *he explained this theory in light of another perspective.* He placed the Freudian paradigm within his own interpretation. It was not as if the Oedipus complex does not exist. But Kohut argued that it could be *better explained* within the conceptual world of a theory of self injury.

Also, classical psychoanalysis asserts that little girls universally experience a narcissistic injury when they discover that they do not possess a penis. This "deprivation" is used to explain why women frequently struggle with self-esteem as they eventually identify with the penis-lacking mother. In fact, their desire to have a child is quite related to this desire to have a penis. This is the portrait painted by classical psychoanalysis.

Here, again, Kohut sees the issue in stark contrast. While he *does* believe that girls go through a certain narcissistic wound when they discover their differences with boys, Kohut seriously questions whether this is a major jolt against a woman's self-esteem. In fact, the desire to have a baby is not reducible to the desire to have a penis. "Penis envy," for Kohut, is not a universal expression of biological deprivation. The so-called desire to have a penis refers to a deeper desire to "fill in" psychological deficits. These deficits were not caused by penis deprivation; instead, they were caused by empathic failures in childhood. The true longing is for those earlier selfobject relationships, relationships that should have affirmed and mirrored a young girl's budding sense of self. The problem, again, is not biological (lack of penis) but psychological (emotional deficits). Rowe and MacIssac state this issue sharply:

Kohut disagrees with the belief that "penis envy," detected in some women in analysis, is a universal expression of a biologically based narcissistic trauma that affects all women equally. Rather than an expression of "biological bedrock," Kohut considers it to be "psychological surface," covering a particular woman's enfeebled and depressed self. Her erotic fantasies of having a penis, or her desire to have one, is thus not an expression of an attempt to make up for a biologically based difference with men, but is evidence of a craving to fill in the psychic deficits that she suffered so perversely at the hands of the unempathic selfobjects of her childhood. Having lost hope of ever attaining the responsiveness of those early mirroring selfobjects, she may turn to erotic fantasies for self-stimulating and self-soothing sensation states that act as a substitute for the missing self structure.[34]

Over and over again, Kohut invites us to look behind the so-called drive and acknowledge the narcissistic wound beneath it. To repeat, for Kohut, drive preoccupations are always an outgrowth of self injury. The drives are a substitute for the deeper need to be prized, affirmed, and recognized for who we really are. Specific drives become problematic because the *entire self* has not been empathically mirrored. As we have seen, this Kohutian point is in profound disagreement with Freudian psychoanalysis. Our problems with excessive fixations on sex and aggressions are byproducts, secondary problems to the more pervasive issue of self injury. They represent deficits to the self, not the chaotic and wild impulses of biological urges. Once again, while Kohut is not denying the existence of destructive impulses, he is questioning the *source* of

them. We will not solve a so-called drive problem until we look at what lies beneath these unruly impulses. And that source is not our biology; it is instead the empathic failures in the psychological worlds out of which we have emerged.

SELF INJURY AND NARCISSISM

If any particular topic put Kohut on the psychoanalytic conceptual map, it was his approach to narcissism. In essence, Kohut went from an exploration of the particular dynamics of narcissistic personality disorder to the conviction that narcissism is a universal struggle, a basic part of human life. Put simply, we *all* have narcissistic issues. It helps very little to condemn and berate narcissists without a deep understanding of the dynamics that perpetuate this condition. Kohut wanted desperately to move away from a moralistic and judgmental condemnation of this condition. Even in psychoanalytic circles, he found a rather condescending and negative attitude toward narcissists. Rather than viewing the narcissist as hopelessly full of him/herself, Kohut wanted to grasp the injuries to the self that propelled the narcissist's grandiosity.

In examining this issue, Kohut came to believe that narcissism has a "line of development" in every person. The problem is *not* who is a narcissist and who is not. The problem is having one's earlier, archaic narcissistic states arrested, fixated, or stuck. The normal course of development is from an early grandiose sense of self to a more reasonable self-perception consistent with one's potential. But for some individuals, this natural development is derailed. The irony is this: unhealthy narcissism does not arise from being indulged; instead, it arises from being ignored. Unhealthy narcissism does not emerge from too much attention; it emerges from too little. Pathological narcissism, while appearing as excessive self-esteem, actually involves a profound inability to regulate self-esteem.

> When we analyze adults who suffer from narcissistic disturbances
> . . . we may get the impression that they were spoiled as children.
> . . . But that's not so. . . . They became fixated on drives because
> their budding selves were overlooked, were not responded to.
> They turned to drive-gratification . . . because they tried to . . .
> escape the horrible feeling that nobody was responding to them.
> Such people may have had mothers who satisfied their drives
> continuously, yet failed to respond with pride and pleasure to the
> child's independent self.[35]

Perhaps another way of putting this is that a child can be "spoiled" in terms of material possessions and lavish treatment while at the same time being psychologically neglected and abandoned. In fact, a good case could be made that many parents attempt to compensate for their psychological unavailability by providing their children with an excessive supply of "things." A lack of attentiveness, mirroring, and genuine connection cannot be erased through lavish gifts and the indulgence of children. Thus, so-called spoiled children, when one looks a deeper level, may well be narcissistically deprived children.

Again, for Kohut, when one's natural, narcissistic childhood needs are met, the natural tendency is to move out of them rather than stay fixated in them. Thus, a central Kohutian conviction is that grandiosity *per se* is not an enemy that must be destroyed. Instead, the point is to transform grandiosity into appropriate ambition. This is *mature narcissism*. The goal is to transform, rather than to eliminate, early grandiosity. If adequately mirrored, this more primitive form of grandiosity will turn into healthy goal-oriented pursuits. Pathological narcissism always refers to the failure to support and integrate the archaic self in its journey toward a mature self. When fixated or stuck, this archaic self manifests itself in some fairly ugly ways: entitlement claims, unrealistic ambitions, arrogance, omnipotence, and the complete domination of others. Yet, amidst this display of self-mastery is a deeply fragile need for others to supply the narcissistic supplies one cannot supply oneself. For Kohut, this process of movement from archaic grandiosity to mature ambition is a natural one *if empathic mirroring is present*. There is no need to attack and dismantle the grandiosity. Empathic understanding will help the grandiosity eventually fade into realistic goals.

It is very important, then, to understand how Kohut radically changed the conversation about narcissism. For Kohut, emotional deprivation freezes the development of mature narcissism. The narcissist is not on some strange and different path from the non-narcissist. Instead, the narcissist has been retained, derailed, or arrested at an earlier stage of development. The grandiosity is still archaic, still childlike, still in need of maturational transformation. But all people travel the narcissism road.

Again, it is not that we must reject our narcissistic needs in order to care for others. We each have a narcissistic line of development, which is not in competition with, and certainly does not eliminate, love for others. Our basic narcissistic needs and the search for adequate selfobjects represent the very foundation of psychological life. Our narcissistic needs are at the core of our self and in lifelong need of responses from the selfobjects in our lives. The self is intricately tied to these responses from others. Beneath our relationship problems with others, according to Kohut, is a deeper disturbance in our narcissistic development. Thus, relationship distress points back to *self* distress. Relationship problems are intimately tied to the quality of our self cohesion. In the same manner that Kohut believed narcissistic injuries were behind our unruly drives, so narcissistic injuries are usually behind our interpersonal conflicts as well. The paradox is this: the best thing we can bring to our relationships with others is solid self cohesion; yet self cohesion depends upon the quality of support in our significant relationships. This, again, is why

Kohut should *not* be accused of fostering an unrealistic view of human autonomy. He identified a lifelong dance between our own narcissistic development and the availability of healthy selfobjects.

In order to see the significance in Kohut's departure from Freud's view of narcissism, perhaps it would be helpful to summarize the key points in Freud and Kohut. Freud and classical psychoanalysis held that all of an infant's libidinal energy is originally directed at him/herself. This is called *primary narcissism.* The infant's thoughts are magical and fantastical as he/she feels omnipotent. The child's early frustrations interrupt these fantasies of omnipotence and grandeur. As infants are unable to achieve gratification through primary narcissism, they turn their libidinal energy toward *outside objects*, thus shifting narcissistic libido to object libido. The parents then become the crucial love objects. This parental attachment and the Oedipal fantasies connected with it present the next developmental crisis. There is a limited amount of libido that can be spent. If we direct it at ourselves, we will have nothing left for anyone else. Thus, self-love is *detrimental* to the development of object love. Love of others involves a movement *away from* self-love. Narcissism, like schizophrenia, involves a regression to an early part of infancy in which self-absorption is dominant. The narcissist, because he or she has not developed object relationships, cannot transfer the emotional content of those relationships onto the psychoanalyst. Because transference is the very backbone of psychoanalysis, those who cannot transfer (including the narcissist) are not "analyzable." Again, narcissists are not good candidates for psychoanalysis because they developed no earlier attachments which can then be transferred onto the analyst. This retreat into a narcissistic orientation involves an avoidance of a more mature involvement with the outside world. The focus, in the unlikely possibility that treatment is even possible, must be upon analyzing, exposing, and challenging the narcissist's resistance and grandiosity. This involves the persistent, repetitive confrontation of the narcissist's use of arrogance and entitlement claims.

This traditional Freudian approach to narcissism makes several important clinical and theoretical assumptions: Love of self is disruptive of love for others. Direct confrontation and interpretation are the best method of dealing with narcissism. Supportive therapy that focuses on the underling narcissistic injuries of the patient might very well encourage the narcissist's grandiose delusions. In such a situation, the analyst may be unwittingly colluding with the patient in an ongoing drama of unchecked narcissism.

In contrast, Kohut believes that this Freudian and classic psycho-analytic approach to narcissism is neither accurate nor effective. Again, Kohut does not agree that narcissists are essentially spoiled, that their grandiosity must be punctured, or that their defenses must be challenged, exposed, and interpreted. Kohut held that instead of confrontation and exposure, narcissistic patients first need empathy. While empathy itself does not cure, it opens the door to interpretation, which is the high-est form of empathy. The analyst should focus on the *experience* of the narcissist, an experience that usually involves far more *vulnerability than actual grandiosity*.

As strange as it sounds, the classical Freudian model does not look deeply enough because beneath the grandiose display is a person who often never feels appreciated for him/herself. These narcissistic individu-als are often extensions of their parent's own narcissistic desires. We do not need to simply measure how much attention a child receives, but instead examine what *kind* of attention it is. For instance, some narcis-sistic parents frequently overstimulate their children's grandiosity while remaining oblivious to who their children really are. Healthy narcissism involves a parental response to the child's innate sense of energy, great-ness, and perfection. It also involves a parental offering of his/herself as a selfobject whom the child can "look up to" and idealize. And finally, it involves a demonstration that the child is in many ways similar to the parent (thus continuing the alterego bond). Stephen A. Mitchell and Margaret J. Black, in their book *Freud and Beyond*, state this very well:

> How does the child emerge from these childhood narcissistic states? Not, Kohut came to believe, by confronting their unreal-istic features. The child who is swooping around the living room in his Superman cape needs to have his exuberance enjoyed, not have his fantasies interpreted as grandiose. The child who believes his mother makes the sun rise in the morning needs to be allowed to enjoy his participation in the divine, not to be informed of his mother's diminutive status in the universe. These early narcissistic states of mind contain the kernels of healthy narcissism; they must be allowed slow transformation on their own, Kohut suggested, simply by virtue of exposure to reality. The child comes to appreciate the unrealistic nature of his views of himself and his parents as he suffers the ordinary disappoint-

ments and disillusions of everyday life: he can't walk through walls, her father cannot decree that her soccer team will always win, and so on. In healthy development, the inflated images of self and other are whittled down, little by little, to more or less realistic proportions. Inevitable yet manageable, optimal frustrations will take place within a generally supportive environment. Against this secure backdrop, the child rises to the occasion, survives the frustration or disappointment, and in the process internalizes functional features of selfobject. For example, he learns to soothe himself, rather collapsing in despair; he comes to experience internal strength despite defeat. Kohut felt that this process, which he termed *transmitting internalization*, is repeated in countless little ways and builds internal structure, eventuating in a secure, resilient self that retains a kernel of excitement and vitality of the original, immature narcissistic states.[36]

Kohut found that narcissistic patients are capable of transference and that these transferences pointed toward earlier, unmet childhood needs. Like other analysts, Kohut began to understand the analytic relationship to be in many ways a recreation of the early parent-child relationship. But Kohut felt that traditional analysis had *not* understood the nature of narcissistic transferences, which Kohut later called "selfobject transferences." One of these transferences, as we have seen, is the *mirroring* transference. Here the narcissistic patient wants the analyst to be a perfect mirroring mother or primary caregiver. The patient needs his/her excitement, perception, disappointment, and so on to be understood. What the patient was previously denied, and is currently looking for, are affirming, applauding responses for his/her perceptions, achievements, insights, and actions. This makes the experience of the narcissistic patient more real. Another transference is the *idealizing* transference in which the patient idealizes the analyst and feels strong by virtue of his/her connection with the analyst. And finally, there is an *alterego* transference in which the patient wants to feel an essential "likeness" with the analyst. All three of these transferences re-create what Kohut believed to be a part of the development of healthy self-regard. As Mitchell and Black tell us, these transferences look quite different than the traditional Oedipal transferences:

> None of these transferences are much like the oedipal transferences that are the hallmark of classical psychoanalysis. Most striking is that interpretation is, Kohut found, disastrous. If the

analyst interprets (in the mirroring transference) that the patient's self-perceptions are inflated and need to be renounced
(in the idealizing transference) or that the patient's view of the
analyst is inflated and needs to be abandoned or (in alter ego
transference) that the presumed likeness between patient and
analyst is defensive or illusory, self-esteem collapses and either
a demoralizing sense of emptiness and futility or a rageful out-
pouring ensues (p. 161).

Again, the *key Kohutian point* here is that if these transferences
are not challenged and immediately interpreted, but instead allowed
to develop, there will *not* be a further regression or deeper narcissistic
fixation, as classical analysis suggests. The classical analysis would argue
that Kohut is simply supporting the patient's infantile grandiosity and
colluding in the perpetuation of self-absorption. Yet Kohut disagrees.
He found that his patients needed this experience from him in order
to move out of it. This nurturing, mirroring experience addresses the
narcissistic injuries that keep these patients from moving forward. As
a result, a more robust, yet realistic, sense of self emerges. The analytic
situation replays an earlier experience of narcissistic injury.

Thus, once again, Kohut places the emphasis on the injurious impact
of the child's early psychological environment rather than the primitive,
grandiose urges arising from within. In fact, our anxious concern for
self-protection creates more problems than our so-called drives of sex
and aggression. Out-of-control sex and aggression are, as we have seen,
disintegrative byproducts. By the time the Oedipal issue rolls around, the
child is often *already* dealing with a very wounded sense of self. Self injuries are deeper than conflicts. Aggression and rage reveal an underlying vulnerability that must be addressed. Aggression is a reactive form
of self-protection. Thus, Kohut offers a theory of deficit rather than a
theory of conflict.

CONCLUSION

In this chapter, we have contrasted two views of the human condition.
One view, which rather persistently focuses on the problem of unhealthy,
innate tendencies and destructive drives, can be seen in the Augustinian
and Freudian portrait of human nature. For this orientation, our primary
problem is the inherent inclinations within us, which push us toward
destructive ends.

In contrast to this Augustinian/Freudian model, Kohut argues that the source of our problems is not in our inherited nature, but instead, in the emotional deficits and psychological injuries that occur in early life. While Kohut does not deny the severity of humanity's destructiveness, he does not think it is rooted in our biology or basic nature. It is instead a result of injuries to the self.

We also examined Kohut's conviction that narcissism is a universal concern. The issue, once again, is not whether or not we have narcissistic struggles, but whether or not our narcissistic development has been ruptured, arrested, and stuck in its early archaic form. The shaming of narcissism, for Kohut, is completely ineffective. Narcissism needs to be reconnected to early trauma and self injury if it is to be adequately grasped.

The question may persist as to whether Kohut's "softer" view of the human condition does justice to the traditional theological idea of sin. It is to this important question that we now turn.

END NOTES

1. Strozier, *Heinz Kohut*, 300.
2. Kohut, *Chicago Institute Lectures*, 67.
3. Strozier, "Heinz Kohut's Struggles with Religion, Ethnicity, and God," 170.
4. Strozier, *Heinz Kohut*, 217–18.
5. Kohut, *Chicago Institute Lectures*, 199–201.
6. Ibid., 208–9.
7. Gay, *Understanding the Occult*, 41.
8. Kohut, *Chicago Institute Lectures*, 66.
9. Ibid., 200.
10. See Browning, *Fundamental Practical Theology*; and Browning and Cooper, *Religious Thought and the Modern Psychologies*.
11. Augustine, *City of God*, 573.
12. Ibid., 571.
13. Ricoeur, *Symbolism of Evil*, 239.
14. Watts, *Beyond Theology*, 63.
15. Weatherhead, *Christian Agnostic*, 286.
16. Ibid., 274.
17. Tillich, "Impact of Pastoral Counseling on Theological Thought," 15.
18. Freud, *Civilization and Its Discontents*, 69.

19. Tillich, "Theological Significance of Existentialism and Psychoanalysis," 88–89.

20. Ibid., 89–91.

21. Niebuhr, "Human Creativity and Self-Concern in Freud's Thought"; Cooper, *Reinhold Niebuhr and Psychology*.

22. Greenlee, "Kohut's Self Psychology and Theory of Narcissism," 114.

23. Miller, *Using Self Psychology in Child Psychotherapy*, 12.

24. Cooper, *Reinhold Niebuhr and Psychology*.

25. Irenaeus, *Against Heresies*, quoted in Burns, *Theological Anthropology*, 23.

26. Ireneaus, *Against Heresies*, quoted in ibid., 25.

27. Quoted in Strozier, *Heinz Kohut*, 380.

28. Rowe and MacIsaac, *Empathic Attunement*, 72–74.

29. See especially Browning and Cooper, *Religious Thought and the Modern Psychologies*, ch. 4.

30. Kohut, *Analysis of the Self*, 298.

31. Freud, *Interpretation of Dreams*, 261.

32. Dobson, "Freud, Kohut, Sophocles: Did Oedipus Do Wrong?"

33. Ibid.

34. Rowe and MacIssac, *Empathic Attunement*, 89–90.

35. Kohut, *Chicago Institute Lectures*, 208–9.

36. Mitchell and Black, *Freud and Beyond*, 159–60.

3

Kohut and the Seven Deadly Sins

... the intensity or the lengths to which people will go to balance a shaky self-esteem is enormous.

—Heinz Kohut[1]

... denunciations of narcissism by theologians rarely include any acknowledgment that the narcissism label does not only apply to others, but applies to all of us, regardless of age, gender, or social status.

—Donald Capps[2]

IN THE PREVIOUS CHAPTER, we contrasted Kohut with a broad stream of the Western tradition that has focused on the darker dimensions of the human condition. From this darker perspective, something is inherently wrong with us. Our destructiveness, violence, and capacities for evil emerge from an inherited blueprint that is self-seeking and corrupt. In contrast to this Augustinian/Freudian emphasis on out-of-control drives, we examined the more optimistic view of Kohut. While acknowledging the human capacity for destructiveness, Kohut refused to see that destructiveness as a part of our basic nature. Instead, psychological deprivations and distortions promote the human dilemma. The problem, again, is not endogenous to the human condition.

In contrasting these two perspectives, the question that quickly emerges is whether Kohut's more optimistic portrait of the human condition can really account for humanity's long history of violence and cruelty. Again, Freud answered this question by pointing toward the inherent and ineradicable conflicts and drives within us. "Outside" conflict is a manifestation of "inside" conflict. *Of course* there is destructiveness all around us; there is destructiveness *within* us. As we have seen, Kohut refused to locate this destructiveness within our biological makeup.

Charles Strozier is well aware that Kohut's view of the human condition is often seen as "too soft."

> Perhaps the most common criticism of Kohut's work is that he fails to deal with aggression adequately. In his emphasis on empathy, so the argument goes, Kohut directed attention away from human evil and the violent potentials in the self that it is essential to grasp and confront if we are to understand the astonishing capacity of humans to engage in war, persecution, torture, abuse, and ordinary, garden-variety cruelty. For Kohut, it is said, things are sugarcoated. One loses entirely the crucial insights Freud gained into the "seething cauldron" of id impulses. Even if one concedes, as most observers now would, that classical psychoanalysis as a form of treatment is only clinically relevant in radically modified form, Freud as a philosopher of the human soul properly understood and appreciated the varied forms of aggression. Kohut is uplifting, the critics say, but in the end, superficial, naïve, best fit for the surface, where Americans mostly dwell psychologically.[3]

Was Kohut naïve and overly optimistic about the human condition? Psychologically speaking, did he have an inflated view of human potential? Theologically speaking, did he have no place in his system for the traditional concept of sin? As we look around us at a world full of violence, destruction, and excessive desires, we must ask, "How did we get this way?" If every theological system is stuck with the problem of theodicy (How does a loving, powerful God allow evil?), then every psychological theory is stuck with the problem of anthropodicy (How can human beings do such destructive things to each other?). Kohut's consistent answer to this question points in the direction of need deprivation rather than innate destructive drives. We are certainly not suggesting that Kohut's perspective provides an exhaustive understanding of the highly complex notion of sin in Western theology. Nevertheless, his analysis of the human condition offers fresh and provocative insights into the concept of sin.

As we examine a Kohutian perspective on the classic seven deadly sins, some central themes will emerge. It will be important to see that early injuries in life propel one into an attempt at self-restoration. As we shall see, much of our destructive behavior, while harmful and hurtful to ourselves and others, is often an attempt to *resolve, compensate for, and heal* injuries we have encountered. But it is not just injuries we have already experienced that can provoke unfortunate behavior; it is also the *threat of potential injuries* that shape our actions. Both real injuries and the threat of injury can push us into damaging self-protective maneuvers. The fear of self fragmentation is very strong. Put more simply, human beings can do ugly things when they feel that they are "coming undone." Yet this behavior, in spite of its destructiveness, is usually an attempt to preserve, protect, and restore the self. For Kohut, sin is very closely related to the feeling of falling apart. He frequently refers to this as "disintegration anxiety." When this occurs, individuals attempt, often frantically, to hold themselves together. Many of these methods of trying to hold themselves together *will look like* destructive innate drives. It will always be tempting to simply condemn these actions as innately perverse, inherently wicked, or intentionally destructive. Yet, ironically, some of the most unbalanced things we do are attempts to achieve balance. Perhaps this should be stated even stronger: Kohut would argue that every act of trying to keep the self safe, even when it is a distorted act, is an expression of a self that seeks wholeness, balance, and healing. The self may be choosing some very poor means of achieving that balance, but balance is nevertheless sought. The self is trying to correct the afflictions it already feels or protect itself from the possibility of future injuries.

When the painful threat of unacceptability enters the self's awareness, it is then tempted to engage in a wide variety of methods to regain a sense of self-esteem. This crack in the self's sense of acceptance is inevitable and universal. This typically provokes an attempt to find legitimacy or to "act out" this sense of illegitimacy on the world. In both cases, the injuries to the self go unhealed. What is needed is grace, the deep sense of "accepting our acceptance" as Paul Tillich frequently put it. The beginning of the self's restoration may indeed be a very painful recognition of how all the methods at self-justification have not worked. In fact, these attempts at self-justification have often been hurtful to the self and others. The painful lesson is that once the self has developed its sense of unacceptability, the self cannot, in isolation, heal itself. The self needs the affirming nod of another, the experience of being empathically understood by a caring person. These interpersonal expressions of acceptance (horizontal grace) point toward a larger ontological acceptance, which is insured by our Source (vertical grace). When this profound sense of acceptance is experienced, it is possible to move away from some of our destructive and self-sabotaging tendencies. But we must not get the cart ahead of the horse: this sense of grace precedes change. We do not change in order to experience it. Grace meets us in our darkest hours. In the midst of some of our "deadliest" sins, grace offers the possibility of transformation. Encounters with this grace may not be labeled as "theological." Yet it is the conviction of the authors that this grace is ultimately grounded in a horizon of acceptance that underlies interpersonal acceptance.

Thus, as we explore the seven deadly sins, it is important to remember that they are not just unfortunate byproducts of self injuries, not just efforts to hold the self together, but also the occasions where transformation can occur. Again, the ultimate Source of this acceptance or grace does not have to be explicitly named in order to be experienced. Perhaps later one will come to a deeper grasp of the true foundation of this acceptance. One may see that this interpersonal acceptance one so desperately needs is part of a much larger framework of acceptance that involves the affirming warmth of God.

DEADLY SINS AND NARCISSISTIC INJURIES

The classification of the seven deadly sins has provided a rich stimulus for much reflection about the human condition in Western intellectual history. A precursor to the idea of deadly sins may have been Tertullian's notion of "unpardonable sins" (c. 200 CE). Eventually, however, these "unpardonable" sins were transformed into the seven "deadly" sins. Evagrius of Pontus, an Egyptian monk, formulated eight deadly sins. John Cassian helped sustain a focus on these eight sins. In the sixth century, Gregory the Great frequently described the seven deadly sins with which we are now familiar: *pride, envy, wrath, lust, greed, gluttony, and sloth.* These seven sins were matched by corresponding virtues. Perhaps many of us associate the seven deadly sins with Dante's *Inferno* or Chaucer's *Canterbury Tales.*

As reflection on the seven deadly sins developed, pride often became known as the primary sin out of which the rest emerged. This follows the Augustinian notion that all other sins occur because of our attempt to replace God as the center of our lives. Pride is our downfall. By elevating ourselves as the center of our own existence, our lives are thrown out of balance and we commit the remaining sins. Self-exaltation is the first, and most devastating, of all the sins.

How might Kohut shed light on this deadly sin of pride? While he would clearly understand self-centeredness, arrogance, or self-exaltation as a central human dilemma, he would ask if there might be something beneath this exaggerated self-estimation. He would argue, in fact, that arrogance is a *byproduct* of injuries to the self, rather than the primary condition of human life. Pride or arrogance is real; it is just not the most basic issue. For Kohut, self-exaltation is an unfortunate outgrowth of injuries to the self. When we act "full of ourselves" a nagging sense of self-doubt operates below the surface. While it is true that children emerge with grandiose agendas as a natural part of human development, these elevated and glorified ambitions, when met with optimal human responses, turn into more modest and healthy goals. They do not *remain* grandiose.

To put it directly, Kohut argues that what we have called "sin" results *not* because of an elevated self-image, but instead, because of narcissistic injuries. In other words, sin is not a natural overflow from an inherently inflated self-portrait. Sin is not simply a matter of a self who has psychologically "gotten too big for its own britches." Instead, sin results from damages to the self, damages that lead to all sorts of compensatory efforts to restore the self's stature. Arrogant pride is one of those compensations. Sin is not a direct outgrowth of human nature; it is instead a distortion of that nature. As Donald Capps puts it, "The grandiose self is a defense against the deflating experience of discovering that one is not, after all, the center of reality, while the depleted or shameful self is an exaggerated response to narcissistic injury, an overreaction to the blow that one has sustained to what was perfectly healthy narcissism."[4] The point is that our natural development of narcissism is not the problem; the problem is the *interruption and wounding* of this natural state of self-interest. The culprit in our lives is not an innate self-centeredness. The problem is the disruption of a natural line of narcissistic development. Disrupted narcissism is what leads to an unhealthy self-preoccupation. Natural and healthy narcissism is not the source of permanent grandiosity. It will eventually turn into the ambition to achieve worthwhile goals. It is wounded or interrupted narcissism which keeps us stuck in grandiosity. Kohut frequently refers to this as "secondary narcissism" because it is a defensive reaction and not a natural inclination of the self.

One of the most interesting theoretical battles in psychoanalytic history concerns the dynamics of grandiosity in narcissism. Here again, we are led back to a drive-vs.-deficit argument. The two pivotal figures in this debate are Kohut and Otto Kernberg. Kernberg's ongoing complaint about Kohut's approach is that it too gentle and does not adequately account for the intensity of narcissistic aggression. Mitchell and Black provide an excellent summary of the key theoretical and clinical differences between Kohut and Kernberg.

> One of the most interesting ideological barriers in the psychoanalytic literature of recent years has been between Kernberg and the self psychologists. It is worth noting some of the issues that divide the two camps, because they reflect the difference between a revisionist position, like Kernberg's, that nevertheless remains loyal to certain basic features of Freudian thought, and a more radical position, like Kohut's, that left Freud's drive theory more completely behind. Kernberg views Kohut's self psychology as deemphasizing the body, sexuality, and especially, aggression. For Kernberg, the central dynamic struggle is between love and hate, and these manifest themselves necessarily in the transference to the analyst. . . . Kohut regarded aggression as well as impulsive sexuality as byproducts of narcissistic injury. In Kohut's model, people strive for self-organization and self-expression. In Kernberg's model, people are torn by powerful passions of love and hate. Kohut saw the narcissist as attempting to protect brittle self-esteem. Kernberg sees the narcissist as contemptuous and devaluing. Kohut thought the analyst should empathically reflect the narcissist's self-experience so that a more consolidated, more robust self could develop. Kernberg believes the analyst should interpret the narcissist's underlying hostility so that more integrated object relations could develop. The tension between these two approaches, often mirror images of each other, has had an invigorating effect on psychoanalytic theorizing and broadened the range of clinical options for practitioners.[5]

While Kohut believes that narcissism is a fixation at an early stage of development, a fixation based on unmet narcissistic needs at an age appropriate time, Kernberg argues that adult narcissism does not point back to a fixation at a normal stage of development. Instead, it is *pathological* or *defensive*.[6] Narcissism is the result of inner conflict powered by unconscious rage against persons who humiliated us or abandoned one as a child. Thus, the adult's "grandiose self" is very different than the child's early narcissism.[7] The grandiose fantasies of small children center on attention and have a more realistic quality. These fantasies can be checked by reality. Further, the child's desire for admiration and attention can co-exist with a genuine love for Mom and Dad. The child has the capacity to trust and depend on the parents as reliable sources of narcissistic supplies. In contrast, adult narcissists don't love or trust others except for quick shots of attention. Also, childhood narcissism can be gratified. The child can enjoy the attention. Conversely, continue Kernberg, adult narcissism can never be satisfied. The adult grandiose self is enormously envious and often seeks to destroy the other simply because he/she appears "better" than oneself. In addition, childhood self-centeredness is warm and engaging. Children "show off" for someone they love. Adult narcissists, on the other hand, may be superficially charming, but they are actually not interested or invested in anyone. Again, they are only interested in temporary narcissistic supplies.

At the risk of overstating the point, Kernberg's theory of narcissism is more harsh than Kohut's. But he thinks it is more realistic. Kernberg does not believe that narcissistic personality disorder results merely from narcissistic frustration of childhood or deprivation of attention. For Kernberg, Kohut does not do justice to destructive rage, envy, and resentment. For Kernberg, we have an innate capacity for rage. That capacity can be awakened to devalue significant objects. Put simply, *we want to destroy the very source we need in order to eliminate our envy.* The grandiose self of adulthood feels powerless and wants to destroy what others give because one hates one's own helplessness. This grandiosity, for Kernberg, must be interpreted. In describing Kohut's view of narcissism, Kernberg states, "his analysis of pathological narcissism is essentially unrelated to any examination of the vicissitudes of aggression."[8] Envy and rage underlie grandiosity. Kernberg's linkage to Melanie Klein is apparent here.

Kernberg stresses the narcissist's need to devalue others. But one might ask, "Why *does* the narcissistic person want to devalue others?" Kohut would answer that it is because they have *been* devalued. They feel unlovable. Because they are unredeemable, they want to bring down the rest of the world to their level. There is enormous loneliness and feelings of abandonment here, an immense yearning for the self's restoration. Thus, a key difference is that Kernberg, on the one hand, believes that while innate aggression may be mobilized by frustration, the aggression is a much deeper, biologically-rooted phenomenon; while for Kohut, on the other hand, excessive aggression is a frustration-reaction and not built into the very fabric of biological being.

Healthy aggression, on the other hand, can be called upon in service for the achievement of our basic goals in life. It is a normal and inevitable component of life. But the type of aggression described by Klein and Kernberg, from Kohut's perspective, is not an inherent part of a person's makeup. It is wounded aggression, injured rage, which acts to restore a sense of balance and repair to the self. Again, even when distorted, unbalanced, or "sinful," these acts often attempt to hold together a crumbling sense of self. They do not naturally flow from our biological nature. Destructive inclinations are not endogenous.

Again, from Kohut's perspective, grandiosity in the child will naturally be archaic and very self-centered. Gradually, in a healthy atmosphere, the child will learn to accept limitations and replace the grandiose exhibitions with ambitions consistent with the nuclear self. However, if this natural movement is interrupted through any form of trauma, the grandiosity may go underground. Once underground, the grandiosity does not have an opportunity to gradually be transformed into appropriate ambitions. The archaic, primitive grandiosity may remain unconscious, but it can nevertheless be quite destructive. In some cases, a wounded individual will expect another person to provide a constant mirror of his or her fragile self. The individual's own self structure is not strong enough to survive without the constant attention from another. As the baby needs to be the gleam in the mother's eye, so the adult needs the ongoing reassurance from another that he or she is noticed and appreciated. The relationship between the adult suffering from a self disorder and others remains very immature as others are considered a part of the self-injured person. The other person has no identity of his or her own. The other person is not unlike an aspect of the injured self's own body. The other is used for specific purposes. When others do not comply, the result can often be narcissistic rage. This involves a profound sense of entitlement to an ongoing focus from another. When this adoration is lacking, the narcissistically wounded person feels ignored, neglected, and abused. The result is rage at the presumed injustice of impoverished attention. This rage must be seen as an outgrowth of a highly fragile, shaky self. In fact, the rage attempts to keep the self glued together. It may feel powerful, but this feeling masks the reality that a sense of "falling apart" or fragmentation is underneath it. In his Chicago Institute Lectures, Kohut describes the narcissist as

> ... an individual in whom the cohesion of the self or the idealized self-object is fragile. The cohesion depends on favorable external circumstances and tends to be more or less severely disturbed, leading to some kind of a fragmentation when circumstances are unfavorable. In other words, it occurs when there are no narcissistic supplies, no narcissistic sustenance or praise or approval, or when the idealizable object does not allow the closeness necessary for merger. Under those circumstances, disintegration takes place.[9]

A fixation at the level of the primitive, grandiose self can have two very defensive outcomes. First, a person may appear to have low self-esteem because the primitive, grandiose self is repressed and unavailable to consciousness. There is little enthusiasm, low self-esteem, and depression. There is often a fear of and anticipation of rejection from others, a fear based on the previous, childhood expressions of grandiosity. Because the grandiosity is repressed, it cannot be properly channeled into healthy ambition and an enthusiasm for the achievement of goals. Kohut sometimes called this repression of grandiosity the "horizontal split." It is important to understand, however, that this archaic, grandiose self has not left the psyche. Grandiosity is still present and can sometimes come bursting forth with rage when it feels ignored or unrecognized. Low self-esteem, depression, and limited ambition seem to dominate, but the grandiose self can still come forth with a strong reaction to injury. The grandiosity is always in the background. Again, the tragedy here is that because all forms of grandiosity are repressed, they cannot be transformed into healthy ambitions. The person thus suffers from low energy, low enthusiasm, and a sense of self depletion. The key, then, is not to deny, ignore, or try to eliminate the grandiose self; the point is to transform its grandiosity into worthwhile, realistic goals for which it can strive.

Second, for other individuals, the grandiose self is in the foreground. In other words, they appear full of themselves and have no awareness of how repugnant this grandiosity may appear to others. There is no repression of grandiosity here. It is "out there" for the world to see. Thus, some individuals are out of touch with their repressed grandiosity; for others their grandiosity is apparent but they is ignorant of its unpleasant impact on others. This is what Kohut frequently called "disavowal." The person is aware of his or her actions but denies that these actions are overbearing or inappropriate. This is the person who always needs to be the center of the conversation, the focus of the party, or the one who seems intoxicated with him- or herself.

The Kohutian point can be straightforwardly stated: The rejections of age-appropriate narcissistic needs leads to the fixation of those needs. Without the appropriate mirroring at an age-appropriate time, a person grows up mirror-hungry and preoccupied with a very unsettled self-image. The calming, nurturing, soothing voice of the caretaker has not been internalized. Consequently, one must forever look for mirrors and adoring audiences. For Kohut, beneath all the narcissistic demands is a sad and lonely, highly fragile self, desperately needing others to perform psychological functions he or she does not possess. A person cannot internalize what was never offered. Hence he or she is missing the vital ability to regulate his or her self-esteem. In other words, the ups and downs of self-esteem are completely in the hands of outsiders. While healthy selfobjects are important and necessary in all self-esteem maintenance, injured selves are forced to over-rely on outsiders for all soothing, affirmation, and confidence. The ability to self-sooth, to attend to one's own sense of fragmentation, or to offer one's self an empathic understanding are simply not present. One's need for others takes on a desperate quality.

Perhaps an analogy might be helpful in understanding the process of self-esteem regulation. The goal, as we have seen, is to develop a more coherent sense of self. This coherent sense of self is very much like having a good set of shocks on one's automobile. If one does not have good shocks, various bumps and potholes in the road can be very disorienting, disturbing, and raise the possibility of a wreck. With solid shocks, the potholes, which are inevitable, can be absorbed without excessive disequilibrium. One does not feel as if one's car is falling apart when the pothole is encountered. Instead, the bump can be absorbed, noticed, and one can move on. This is not to say that the road will be smooth and one will not notice the bumps. Yet, the car is now sturdy enough to handle the road hazards.[10]

Take, for instance, the experience of defeat. A sense of defeat can lead to temporary deflation or depression as one figures out how to reinvest one's ambitions differently. Yet for those who lack self-esteem regulation, defeat can result in a morbid depletion and a feeling of devastation. One may feel utterly demoralized. However, for many, even after this demoralization, the narcissistic injury will trigger archaic forms (rather than mature forms) of self-regulation. One will be tempted to engage in arrogance, conceit, or archaic grandiosity as massive cover-ups and compensations for the feeling of depletion. It is important to note the self-preserving functions of these prideful expressions.

So, Kohut would in no way discount the appearance of grandiosity, arrogance, conceit, and all the things we associate with the traditional deadly sin of pride. But he would interpret them as byproducts of self injury, as compensations of a fragmenting self. Pride is pervasive and real. But we deal with it more adequately by pointing toward its underlying insecurity and lack of self cohesion than by railing against narcissism.

The second deadly sin is envy. In his book on the seven deadly sins, Solomon Schimmel defines envy as "the pain we feel when we perceive another individual possessing some object, quality, or status we do not possess."[11] While jealousy is often used interchangeably with envy, the two can be distinguished. Jealousy has the quality of being afraid someone will take what we have; envy involves wanting what someone else has. Envy "can't stand it" that someone has something we do not. Envy always seems to involve an unfavorable comparison of ourselves with another. Somehow the accomplishments of others bring to light our own sense of inferiority. Or as Donald Capps puts it, "Envy forms when we believe that the other person's advantage or possession diminishes or brings disgrace on us. Once we believe that, we try to divest those we envy of their advantage, usually trying to 'pull the other person down.'"[12] In some cases, envy can reach vicious, destructive proportions. We may want to "bring down" those whom we envy. We may not be able to stand it that they are better than we are in some aspect of life. Somehow *their* *success triggers a sense of* failure. We see their accomplishments as less a statement about *their ability* and more about *our lack of ability*. This provokes rumination over our own deficiencies and does not allow us to appreciate the accomplishments of others or even our own accomplishments. Because this acknowledgment of our deficiency is so painful, we may quickly move toward denouncing another's so-called success as a sham. They didn't *really* achieve what others think they achieved.

Some may suggest that envy is based on a cognitive distortion that needs to be addressed. We may indeed be telling ourselves that because someone accomplishes more than we have accomplished in a given area, we are therefore worthless. Our own self-commentary is creating the problem. Therefore, we need simply to adjust our thinking process and see the distortion for what it is. We can *both* acknowledge someone's accomplishment and *not* think negatively about ourselves.

Kohut, however, would suggest that while we examine our cognitive distortion we also need to reflect on the narcissistic injuries that accompany this cognitive distortion. In other words, it may be quite difficult to simply eradicate our envy without understanding the precarious self state beneath it. Stated differently, those with a coherent and healthy sense of self have far less need or tendency to be envious. Those with a more secure sense of self can applaud the accomplishments of others without it being a serious challenge to a very fragile self. Other people's success does not have to be a commentary on our own deficiency. This is what St. Paul urges us toward when he says that love does not rejoice over wrong. The other person does not have to be deflated for us to become inflated.

Melanie Klein, a highly influential psychoanalyst who followed Freud's drive theory and death-instinct model, argued that envy is rooted in constitutional aggression. In other words, Klein believed there is a biological basis for our problems with envy. It is a natural outflow of our aggressive nature. For Klein, people resent the very individuals who can help them, and hence, often want to destroy those helpers. Envy hates its own dependency. For instance, the very idea that an analyst might be able to help the envious patient makes the patient want to discount or devalue the analyst's interpretation. The analyst reminds the patient over and over of his/her helplessness. The patient cannot stand the idea that the analyst has this power over him/her. Whether or not the analyst's interpretation is simply dismissed or ferociously assaulted, the analyst represents something beyond the patient's control, and hence, needs to be denounced. The envy experienced emerges from a biological tendency to destroy—even if it means destroying the very thing a person needs.

Contrary to Klein, Kohut refuses to root envy in our innate disposition and instead sees it connected to self injuries. Envy is an unfortunate attempt to repair narcissistic injury. The destructive aggression emphasized by Klein, and then later developed by Kernberg, does not represent a direct outgrowth of our drives. Further, it does not explain the core of our envy. Envy, like destructive aggression, is a byproduct of narcissistic wounding. The *psychological* experience of narcissistic injuries, rather than the *biological* struggle with an innate destructive drive, is the seat of our struggle. We feel envious, even destructively envious, because another's accomplishment brings on a sense of our own self fragmentation. *A person with a coherent sense of self does not have to experience this level of envy.* It is a wounded, fragmented, insecure self which needs to devalue and destroy the abilities of others. We are not *doomed* to hate our dependency on others. A mature and healthy sense of self can recognize that we need self-selfobject relationships all our lives. This sense of dependency does not *have* to be threatening. A destructive sense of envy is always preceded by a sense of "coming undone" and poor self-cohesion. Stated simply, the more "together" we feel, the easier it will be to appreciate the accomplishments of others. But these accomplishments bother us when we do not feel secure. *Thus, the narcissistic injury problem is deeper than, and prior to, the envy problem.*

The third deadly sin is wrath. This must be distinguished from ordinary anger, anger that can be used in the service of healthy striving rather than destructiveness. Wrath, or what we might call "rage," is an exaggerated, intoxicated anger that is out of control and unproductive. This is not the kind of assertive anger that can lead to greater social justice or personal fulfillment. This is not a humanity-serving anger. Instead, it is an unruly, chaotic experience that can easily lead to violence. Kohut understood this as narcissistic rage. Wrath, from Kohut's perspective, needs to be connected to narcissistic woundedness. Strozier, once again, elegantly summarizes Kohut's perspective.

> There can be no rest for someone who has suffered a narcissistic injury, which suggests the origin of rage in perceived psychological injuries like ridicule, contempt, and conspicuous defeat. The sequence here is important. The narcissistically vulnerable person responds with heated imagination to an otherwise minor slight, which in turn provokes a state of fragmentation that unravels the self. Rage is the byproduct. For Freud, it is worth noting, the sequence is exactly the opposite. We are constantly stirred by aggressive impulses that are ultimately of a biological origin and are only contained by the thin defensive wall erected in the process of ego development. It is only natural that things break though at times. In fact, the capacity to "sublimate" aggressive drive urges is a rare gift. The human norm for Freud is aggression and violence.

His is a grim view of human nature and his theory a grand elaboration of his dark pessimism.[13]

As Strozier goes on to remind us, Kohut sees rage as involving a
disproportion between the perceived injury and the revenge desired.
It exaggerates the hurt and has no empathy for the offender. The rage
becomes obsessional. Again, it must be remembered that for Kohut, rage
is very different from mature aggression. Mature aggression works in
service of the self. It is a natural capacity that aids in the strengthening of the self. Rage, on the other hand, is an outgrowth of narcissistic
injury and represents a fragmented and wounded self's attempt to exact
revenge.

One of the authors of this book remembers an experience as an undergraduate in which a professor used his presentations to a lecture hall
of over 300 people as an opportunity to perform on stage. Somewhat in
love with the sound of his own voice and the quality of his own opinions,
he would use class time as a means of trying to impress students with the
extent of his insight. He was mirror-hungry, and his students were a cap-
tive audience. During one lecture, an undergraduate student happened
to glance down at the school newspaper to get some information. Right
in the middle of a sentence, the professor pointed this student out and
immediately ordered him out of the lecture hall. Keep in mind that this
student was in no way interfering with the lecture in terms of talking or
distracting other students. Yet, for the professor it was outrageous that
the student did not offer a set of adoring eyes for the entire class period.
Rage quickly emerged as the professor demanded the student to leave
the class. A so-called empathic failure had pushed the professor over the
edge and thrown him into a state if self fragmentation. The fact that hun-
dreds of other students were listening attentively made no difference.
This one particular student was not functioning as a mirroring other.
Thus, this slight touched his vulnerable grandiose self and he erupted
with narcissistic rage.

The next three deadly sins are lust, greed, and gluttony. We place
these three sins together here because they share a very similar dynamic.
They all have to do with inordinate desire. While differing in their focus,
these three excessive tendencies share an overlapping issue. Put simply,
they use a particular thing (sex, money, food, etc.) as a means of compensating for something that is lacking within. For Kohut, these out-of-
control desires are based on an attempt to reduce the tensions of self

fragmentation. We use as selfobjects specific substances or activities that we believe will help hold us together. But these substances and addictive activities make poor selfobjects because they are not able to help the self with its deepest needs. In fact, these substances or activities were never intended to provide this function. Compulsive eating, drinking, gambling, sex, or any other activity is not equipped to heal the fragmented self. These things are temporary but poor means of achieving self-esteem.

The word that best describes problematic dynamics of lust, greed, and gluttony is "addiction." While it is important to understand the biochemical roots of addiction, there is also an important psychological function that addiction seeks to fulfill. This function has to do with holding together a fragmenting self. Lacking an important self-selfobject relationship, we can sometimes use a substance or a mood-altering experience to soothe our troubled internal state. Kohut provides a very insightful comment about how we use addictive experiences in attempt at self-repair. They become a temporary means of holding the self together.

> The addict . . . craves the drug because the drug seems to him capable of curing the central defect in his self. It becomes for him the substitute for a self-object which failed him traumatically at the time when he should still have had the feeling of omnipotently controlling its responses in accordance with his needs as if it were part of himself. By ingesting the drug he symbolically compels the mirroring self-object to soothe him, to accept him. Or he symbolically compels the idealized self-object to submit to his merging into it and thus to his partaking of its magical power. In any case the ingestion of the drug provides him with the self-esteem which he does not possess. Through the incorporation of the drug he supplies for himself the feeling of being accepted and thus of being self-confident; he craves the experience of being merged with a source of power that gives him the feeling of being stronger and worthwhile. And all these effects of the drug tend to increase his feeling of being alive, tend to increase his certainty that he exists in the world. . . . It is the tragedy of . . . these attempts at self-cure that . . . they cannot succeed. . . . no psychic structure is built, the defect in the self remains.[14]

Addiction points toward our attempt to heal self fragmentation through a soothing drug, comforting food, a nurturing sense of wealth, or mood-altering sex. All of these things demonstrate an attempt to find something that can make up for the self's weak or missing capacities of self-regulation. Again, the addiction removes the tension long enough to be bearable—at least temporarily. The bottle, the pills, the sex, the money, the food—these are the "fixes" we need. We lack an ability to regulate our tensions without these things. As Kohut puts it:

> It is the structural void in the self that the addict tries to fill— whether by sexual activity or by oral ingestion. And the structural void cannot be filled any better by oral ingestion than by any other forms of addictive behavior. It is the lack of self-esteem of the unmirrored self, the uncertainty about the very existence of the self, the dreadful feeling of the fragmentation of the self that the addict tries to counteract by his addictive behavior.[15]

It is not at all uncommon to hear recovering addicts talk about a "relationship" with their drug of choice. It is also not uncommon to hear compulsive eaters talk about a "relationship" with the food they digest. The same can be said for money, sex, and other matters. What do they mean by this? It would seem, from Kohut's perspective, that the drug performs a temporary but ultimately destructive function of self-soothing. The addictive experience *seems* to the addict to help hold his/her world together. Even when life is coming undone, the addictive experience seems to provide coherence. The relationship with the drug, the food, or the money becomes the most important relationship in the addict's life.

A lust for sex, an inordinate desire for money, and an insatiable craving for food are not based on our unruly drives; instead, they are based on deficits. They are attempts to build solid walls of self structure. Yet they are bound to fail. Few could put this as well as Kohut, himself:

> ...all these quasi-magical, instantly satisfying, archaic attempts to replace structure building are like eating when one has a gastric fistula. The eating simply does not satisfy one's need for nour-ishment, it doesn't really feed one, it doesn't build up internal structure. This is the terrible drivenness of the perversion. It is not because the erotic drive is so unmanageable; the erotic drive is really not so unmanageable. The drivenness is the drivenness of a person without structure, who tries to acquire structure by means that just do not and cannot build up structure. As I said, it is like eating with a gastric fistula—the ingested food comes right out of the stomach again without ever remaining in the body long enough to be digested and transformed into absorbable

food substances or psychologically transformed into the digestible form that leads to what I call transmuting internalization.[16]

In spite of the fact that lust, greed, and gluttony have such destructive ramifications, there is also a sense in which they represent a sad and pathetic attempt to supply the self with its cohesion. They are poor attempts to regulate self-esteem. They are fall-outs of an injured self looking for glue to hold it together. The temporary comfort, the soothing "other," will not persist. Instead, one will return to an insatiable need for more and more.

Thus, rather than viewing these tendencies as another example of inherent drives out of control, drives which must be confronted and tamed, we might want to see them as rather pitiful attempts to "fill in" self structure. Of course the behavior can be obnoxious. Of course the addictive pattern can be destructive. Of course the addict must be challenged to quit. But even when one stops the behavior, the question of the injured self still looms before us. The key is to begin a process of structure building. Excessive sex, food, or money will not build this structure.

The last of the seven deadly sins is sloth. Sloth is perhaps a sin of omission more than one of commission. We saw in the last chapter that Kohut made a distinction between "guilty man" and "tragic" man. The sin of sloth is more associated with tragic man. This is the sin of unfulfilled potential, of "missing the mark" of the self's mature, transformed goals. For Kohut, a healthy self is an enthusiastic self on its way to fulfilling its nuclear ambitions. Ambition, for Kohut, is always a more mature and transformed form of grandiosity. In early psychological experience, a basic design or nuclear self begins to emerge. Fulfillment necessitates the actualization of these potentials.

For Freud, sloth refers to a tendency toward inertia, an ever-present inclination, because, as he frequently said, organic life seeks to return to inorganic life. Sloth represents a slow, less dramatic form of the death instinct. Sloth, then, is intrinsic to our nature. It is a nagging possibility that invites us toward a passive resignation of life.

For Kohut, on the other hand, sloth is not natural to us. It is an outgrowth of empathic failure and self injuries. Sloth points toward a self that is not achieving its nuclear program goals. It leaves us feeling deflated, defeated, and unable to soothe and motivate ourselves. It emerges in the absence of healthy selfobjects.

Sloth involves a depletion of the energy and enthusiasm we need in order to complete our ambitions. The slothful person has no motivation, no sense of vitality for life. Slothful individuals have, in a sense, given up on the possibility of finding psychologically healthy and affirming sources of nourishment. Their internal deficits and lack of self structure sink them into inactivity. They lack one of the key ingredients in Kohut's understanding of mental health: enthusiasm for the self's goals and ambitions.

SIN AND SELF FRAGMENTATION

Our brief examination of the seven deadly sins from a Kohutian perspective helps us see the relationship between sin and self fragmentation. Again, rather than being a constitutionally rooted force toward evil, sin seems to be more of a byproduct of self fragmentation. Perhaps, once again, this is why Kohut understood the grace of God as the "glue" that holds us together. Sin has to do with the feeling of "coming undone" or "falling apart"—fragmentation anxiety. This anxiety, as Kierkegaard and Reinhold Niebuhr said so frequently, is the breeding ground of sin. Feeling anxious, feeling insecure, feeling as if we are falling apart—these experiences can produce some very destructive behavior. But again, it is wrong, according to Kohut, to assume that these destructive tendencies emerge naturally or essentially from our nature. The problem is not in our nature; the problem is anxiety, self fragmentation, and injuries to the self, which produce our most destructive thinking and behavior. Ultimately, sin is that which distorts our created nature and keeps our nuclear self from its deepest expression. Sin, once again, is "missing the mark" of our authentic humanity. It is woven into our lives through the self injuries we experience. Because of this sense of self-alienation and self fragmentation, we all too frequently prize the wrong things, give infinite devotion to finite objects, look for self-soothing in the wrong places, and deny the significance of our ultimate selfobject, God. Put simply, we add to and perpetuate our estrangement problem.

Kohut once said, "There are some shortcomings in your own personality that you make your peace with and you know that they won't change in this life anymore; you'll just have to wait for the next one for that."[17] This deep sense of acceptance, amidst the awareness of deficiency, is what the experience of grace means. Grace helps restore the unity of the self. And this sense of grace can come at unexpected times and in unsuspecting places. Kohut's friend William Kelly remembers Kohut saying, "The grace of God is the unsolicited kindness of strangers."[18] Indeed. While self fragmentation and estrangement seem so pervasive, perhaps grace has the final word.

END NOTES

1. Kohut, *Kohut Seminars on Self Psychology and Psychotherapy*, 32.
2. Capps, *Depleted Self*, 4.
3. Strozier, *Heinz Kohut*, 249.
4. Capps, *Depleted Self*, 28.
5. Mitchell and Black, *Freud and Beyond*, 180.
6. Kernberg, *Borderline Conditions and Pathological Narcissism*, 270–82.
7. Ibid., 272–73.
8. Ibid., 270.
9. Kohut, *Chicago Institute Lectures*, 37.
10. This illustration of automobile shocks and self-regulation was suggestion to us by psychoanalyst Jule Miller, MD.
11. Schimmel, *Seven Deadly Sins*, 57.
12. Capps, *Deadly Sins and Saving Virtues*, 41.
13. Strozier, *Heinz Kohut*, 251.
14. Quoted in Levin, *Treatment of Alcoholism and Other Addictions*, 325–26.
15. Kohut, *Restoration of the Self*, 197.
16. Kohut, *Chicago Institute Lectures*, 256–57.
17. Ibid., 18.
18. Psychoanalyst William Kelly remembered and reported Kohut's comment to Terry Cooper at the St. Louis Psychoanalytic Institute.

4

A New Pastoral Care Orientation for Parishioners

S TUDENTS IN SEMINARY ARE taught how to "think theologically." More is required than just a pious spirit. Clergy need a theological template, a set of perspective-giving tools by which the activities of human life (once symbolized by the newspaper) can be understood from various theological viewpoints (once symbolized by the Bible). In ongoing parish work, pastors typically need to refer to the theological template. They have to consciously apply it rather than having so thoroughly internalized the template that they automatically "think theologically."

We believe that pastors also need to learn to "think psychologically." More is required than just a caring spirit. Seminary students as well as active pastors would benefit from a psychological template, a set of perspective-giving tools by which the activities of parishioners can be deeply understood and by which the responses of the pastor can be fittingly shaped.

The reader knows by now that we believe the self psychology perspective of Heinz Kohut is seminal for informing the pastor's observations, understandings, and responses to the selves of parishioners. In the next chapter we will see how the self psychology perspective can shape a pastoral caregiver's involvement with parish selves in various states of fragmentation. In this present chapter we indicate how various pastoral encounters can be understood and responded to more deeply by using the self psychology template.

It may seem artificial to "think psychologically" in this intentional way, but that is what even the most sophisticated therapeutic helpers must do regardless of their psychological orientation. In addition, learning new healing ways takes a deliberate squinting of one's eyes to begin seeing in new ways, along with some awkward steps when trying to apply them. One goal in this chapter, as in this book, is not to make the reader a self psychologist but to make the reader one who grasps the value of "thinking self psychologically." We do this because we believe that as we see the world differently we also inhabit a new lived world, and when we connect with each other with informed, empathic understanding we then relate to each other in new, redeeming ways. That, in short, is grace—grace for the injured self; grace, in truth, for all of us.

A dear friend of one of the authors sent an account of one of his days as a pastor. The friend (who we will call Rev S) gave permission to share that day, with personal data shielded. We now take his pastoral encounters and reflect on them briefly from a self psychology perspective as a means for illuminating both.

> *My itinerary for the day took me to the campus for a 30-minute walk to St. A's (the closest thing we have to a "cathedral" church in the city) for 10 minutes meditation, back home for a quick breakfast with T, prep to be ready to head off to St. J by 9 am; a pre-marital visit with a couple I'll be doing the ceremony for Sept 26; quick consultation with the substitute pianist/organist for the morning; 10:30 service with 90 percent humidity and 42 brave souls; closing up the church by 1 pm; a pastoral visit with a 90-year-old member for 45 minutes; my half-hour drive back toward home from St. J, this time with St. L's health facility as my destination for a 2:30 service—that completed and all the residents heading back to their rooms by 3:30 pm—home with another pastoral visit en-route— a quick stop to a colleague who is disabled/retired, and moving to C at the end of the month; then home by 4 pm—and catching up with T who had picked up my NY Times. Ordered a healthy meal— personal pan pizza from Pizza Hut, and picked that up for our supper; then subjected myself to viewing the Yankees losing for the second time in 14 games—(it really bothers me when my team loses . . .)—practiced the drums for a half hour in the course of the evening; read all but the magazine section of the Times—and finally with somewhat blurry vision, have finally made it into my office— and found myself still determined to send a note back to you.*

PRE-MARITAL VISIT

A seasoned pastor once said, "I'd much rather do a funeral than a wedding. At weddings there are so many 'raging egos' filling the air." He was right. Narcissistic needs tend to be front and center at weddings. Mirroring, idealizing, and alterego hopes/demands become mobilized from the very beginning of wedding preparations. The narcissistic question becomes, "Who is getting married?," which means, "Who is the one expecting to be honored?" We know that often it is the bride in name only, or the couple in name only. Mothers vie for attention. Bridesmaids and groomsmen do. Professional wedding planners often strive for place of honor.

And so do pastors. For example, strong needs for mirroring may incline clergy to "reign" at pre-marital meetings, wedding rehearsals, and weddings themselves. One such mirror-hungry pastor deemed it his responsibility to lecture the couple on sexual morality and to set rigid boundary on what could and could not be done during the ceremony. He chided attendants when they were late for rehearsal, treated camera people with aloofness, and secretly saw himself as the one who "created" the atmosphere by which the service would "be successful." When he felt he was not being responded to appropriately (narcissistic injury) he "asserted his authority" (a form of narcissistic rage). In this process of solidifying his rights, he lost his dignity, lost the almost instinctive respect that people give to pastors in service situations like weddings and funerals.

Effective pastors try to be aware of narcissistic factors from the beginning of their pre-martial counseling. Toward that goal, they can do a "self-check," monitoring their own mirroring, idealizing, or alterego needs in order to minimize the tendency for current or long-standing selfobject yearnings to become improperly elevated at this time. They may also intentionally "fill their self up," engaging in appropriate mirroring, idealizing, or alterego activities outside the wedding event that will sustain their self cohesion and self-esteem during the wedding event. One pastor routinely went for a long run before weddings as a way to be quietly infused with a sense of well-being.

Ministers can also empathically elicit from the couple what tensions have arisen during wedding planning and how they have affected the couple. One young bride, whose self cohesion had always been vulnerable, reacted to wedding tensions with somatic symptoms: she thought she was developing a rash on her back, thought her heart had begun to beat irregularly, and was convinced that a cap on her tooth was falling off. While pastors in such situations do not typically shift from pre-marital counseling to individual counseling, clergy can help such persons momentarily regain self cohesion. They might suggest that the person could be reassured by actually checking out the reality of their symptoms. Clergy can also gently explain that every person, when under constant stress, begins to feel as if they are falling apart to some degree. Similarly, pastors can indicate that tensions can even create unexpected disruptions in the couple's relationship with each other.

At all times, ministers can vocalize, with sincerity, how the couple's vows are the heart of the whole wedding experience, how precious their love is, and how honored the pastor is to be a part of their marriage service. Pastors informed by self psychology strive to provide appropriate mirroring responses for the wedding couple. They seek to structure means for securing those idealizations the couple need. And they respond as receptively as possible to alterego requests that might generate a sense of oneness among those the couple have gathered around them.

CONSULTATION WITH ORGANIST

Pastors and church staff do not interact simply to "do the work of the church." Beneath the scheduling and decision making is the normal effort of all involved to maintain the cohesion of their selves, achieved by establishing ties with each other as their supportive selfobjects. While church polity and denominational requirements may structure how pastor and staff function together, their ongoing psychological relationship is a set of patterned ways in which each attempts to elicit responses to their selfobject needs.

Clergy especially need to be aware of this for a couple of reasons. First, their public role as ascribed authority gives increased opportunity for expression of their narcissistic tendencies. It's harder, for example, for a church-employed organist to ward off an idealization-hungry senior minister who seeks extra time with the calm, reassuring musician than it is for the senior minister to ward off an idealizing, attention-seeking organist. The organist is more vulnerable to repercussions should narcissistic injuries arise. Vulnerability to the power of another's self is the psychological reason that associate pastors tend to feel less general well-being in churches than do senior pastors. Second, pastors tend to forget, or to minimize, the reality that church staff—paid or not—are often parishioners, too. One's pastoral duty is to promote the well-being of the selves of all parishioners.

Clergy can strive to stay empathically attuned to how their actions affect the self-image, and thus self-esteem, of staff members. For example, one minister coming into a new church spoke regularly of "assuming possession" of the church staff, who now "work under me." He repeatedly referred to them as "my staff." But however affectionate such a phrase might seem—"my staff"—and however corporation-like it sounded to talk of people working "under" someone, these orientations were experienced by the staff as patronizing and demeaning (narcissistic injuries). They saw themselves as workers for their particular church, as contributors to the wider church's mission, as servants of God. They did not see themselves as hired supporters of the senior pastor, as minions of his policies and will. Pastors with strong mirroring needs will tend to have trouble with these "other-thinking" staff members whose allegiance is not pastor-focused. Awareness of one's central narcissistic need (mirroring, idealizing, or alterego) and how intense that need is historically and currently can help pastors avoid creating environments that persistently injure them. Whenever a pastor says, or internally thinks, "Mistakes were made, but not by me," that's a resounding clue for a serious self-check.

Pastors can also have their self fortified during stressful times by understanding the disturbing actions of staff/parishioners from a self psychology vantage point. For example, one pastor experienced the classic run-in with a church organist: the church musician insisted that she was the one to pick music for the sake of the church, for what she considered necessary to strengthen the congregation's life—with only scant attention to what the pastor thought. As the pastor approached the organist with other suggestions, and requested some compliance, the organist's self cohesion began to fragment. She now insisted that she was picking music for music's sake, for the elevation and celebration of great music and great composers. The pastor and the congregation should recognize this. As the pastor, aware of her increasing irrational rationalizations, tried to bring the discussion back to singable hymns and church-appropriate preludes, the organist began to fragment even more. She now began to pick music for the sake of her own self, for what she needed to hold herself together. Some bazaar pieces emerged for a while.

Familiarity with self psychology realities helped the pastor remain calm and caring. He refused to let himself begin to tell stories to himself and others about how terrible she was or how she was demeaning his status and authority. He recognized not only her prior state of self weakness but also how her self was unraveling. He had to act to protect the ministry of music, but he did not feel compelled to vilify her—for in spite of her disruptive actions he understood these as desperate, regressive attempts to retain some semblance of being a functioning self. Parishioners need the most empathic understanding precisely at those times when they are most unlikable.

10:30 WORSHIP SERVICE

Preaching potentially threatens the self-esteem of clergy more than any other pastoral duty. The possibility that one will suffer a sharp narcissistic blow is nowhere greater than when the pastor literally and figurative "exposes" the pastor's self from that high perch behind which he or she cannot hide. All ministers from time to time normally experience injuries to their self-esteem when, for example, responses to their preaching are absent, inadequate, or attacking. What minister has not heard: "Your quote from that writer was too long." "You stand too far away from the microphone." "You should be preaching more from the Bible." "I don't know what you are getting at this morning. It was beyond me." When this happens, a minister loses the reassuring sense of being whole, balanced, and strong. Self-confidence crumbles a bit. If the deflation is mild, the pastor may be able to soothe himself or herself by remembering the affirming comments of other parishioners (restoration through mirroring memories), or by remembering revered pastors who also expressed hard times in the pulpit (restoration through idealizing memories), or by remembering that all of us—pastors and parishioners—are just imperfect beings crowding around the feet of Jesus to hear his word (restoration through alterego memories).

If, however, the pastor is chronically vulnerable to selfobject injuries, and responds to slights about preaching with marked depletion or rage, the pastor's need for soothing may become more intense, and more risky. The pastor may take a harsh tone in the pulpit, using a prophetic voice as a veiled means for punishing those who have failed to be receptive to what he considers his fine sermons. Outside the pulpit, the pastor may become involved in sexual affairs as a desperate attempt to elicit powerful narcissistic responses that will ward off the pain of self disintegration and provide a sense of regained vitality. Here sexual affairs are not primarily about sex. They are frantic efforts to hold the pastor's self together.

And so, if a minister prays before preaching, as many routinely do, then at least a silent prayer should be: "Dear God, give me firmness of self that allows me to love and care even in the face of criticism and disappointment."

Clergy can also serve parishioners well by understanding in new ways the impact of their preaching approach. For example, many preachers fill their sermons with moral injunctions, ethical pronouncements, and righteously indignant judgments. They preach against sin and admonish the sinner to seek forgiveness. While a confrontational voice is still a valid preaching approach, ministers can perhaps see this voice in an altered light.

Part of that altered way of seeing is to grasp that people in the pews are not filled so much with guilt as with emptiness. They do not long so much to be cleansed of their sin as they long for assurances that they are not alone. They do not yearn so much for a word of forgiveness that does not touch their great self-doubts as for a word of encouragement that does. Parishioners feel understood, and begin to heal, when they hear words that touch their deepest needs.

Confrontations that call for accountability are a crucial part of preaching, but perhaps they should be pronounced with the empathic goal of protecting the selves of those who hear. The Gospel of John contains the tender story of a woman caught in adultery being brought to Jesus by the litigious crowd ready to inflict the lawful punishment of stoning (John 8:1–11). The woman is not healed, nor restored to her wholeness, by the apparent moralistic admonition of Jesus to "go and sin no more." She is healed, instead, by Jesus standing beside her, protecting her, demonstrating by his words and gestures that she was precious to him and to God. His "go and sin no more" was a way of saying, "Honor your self. Maintain that dignity, that character of being, with which God created you, so that you may feel whole and be proud of yourself as God would be proud of you." And when Jesus confronts the crowd with "You who is without sin be the first to throw a stone at her," he is not slapping them in the face for their grandiosity. Instead, he is trying to awaken them to empathy, to a deeper awareness of their own limitations that makes persons realize that everyone is in need of love and care, that we are all alike. Moreover, these words of Jesus to the crowd protect them from doing something that would further erode their humanity, further fragment their created goodness as selves, for in committing murder they would fracture their own integrity. Violence disguised as righteous indignation injures both the inflicted and the inflictor.

In the same way Jesus preserves his own self, his own integrity. He does not allow a sense of indignation about the woman's adultery to fill his thinking and feeling. He refuses to let a critical self-righteous attitude disrupt the smooth cohesion of his spirit, and so he says to the woman, "Woman, where are they? Has no one condemned you? *Neither do I condemn you.*" Whatever harsh words Jesus uttered to various individuals, it was always with the intention to awaken, protect, and restore their self rather than to condemn their self. And however muddled his own emotions and thinking sometimes became, he always strived to keep a spirit of empathic lovingkindness at the center of his being and doing. We preachers can strive to do the same—in the pulpit and out.

PASTORAL VISIT WITH ELDERLY PARISHIONER

Hopefully ministers have developed an insightful understanding about death and dying. They need such clarity in pastoral situations where death hovers near, such as in pastoral visits with elderly parishioners.

In a previous chapter we noted one view of death espoused by Sigmund Freud, which has influenced a wide range of psychological and theological templates. Freud sneered at the idea of life as anything other than a lonely journey by autonomous beings on a detour toward death. Death is the universal threat, and facing death is a central, universal developmental crisis with which all people must deal. Since life and death are basically autonomous experiences, compassionate commitment to help others is, therefore, psychologically suspect.

Perhaps this perspective on death is one of the reason Freud seemed to lack empathy. In June of 1911 Carl Jung agonized to Freud over the suicide of Johan Honegger, his young patient, friend, and student, of whom he was fond and to whom he planned to entrust all his work. Jung expressed deep regret over his lack of knowledge as a therapist who might have saved his young patient and was clearly grieving. But Freud could only reply, "I think we wear out a few good men," and "I don't think you could have saved Honegger." This reproachful attitude toward a normal narcissistic sentiment (grief over the loss of a loved one) gives some indication of Freud's hard demeanor toward death, which did not incline him to think empathically about another's feelings.[1]

This was not Heinz Kohut's orientation at all. Kohut affirmed, and demonstrated, that we are in it together. There is no such thing being autonomous, completely separate within one's self. We mutually constitute each other. Passionate help of each other is what we are born with, how we become. We begin and end connected through our basic self-selfobject connections. The tragedy is that those connections can be weak, faulty, or harmful.

And neither does Kohut espouse that we are simply on an unfortunate detour toward death. As we will see in the interviews with Kohut to follow, death is not a challenge as it was with Freud. "Existential anxiety" about death is not inevitable, not a universal crisis. Death is not frightening when ones self is living out its values and goals, even when death is imminent or unfair or cruel.

Indeed, Kohut goes even further. Kohut passionately proclaims that our self can expand and become transformed to where our life—to the very end—is experienced as participation in a supra-individual and timeless existence, where death is accepted as an intrinsic part of life. In this most broadly empathic grasp of our existence, deepened wisdom, humor, and joy are forefront experiences of everyday living and the supports that help preserve our sense of mastery over the finitude of our self and the approach of our impending end.

This can be the inspiring understanding of death that a minister brings to pastoral visits with elderly parishioners. It can fortify the pastor as he or she must repeatedly face those who are dying. It can also serve as a reminder that when people express a fear of death the underlying cause is a fear of living; or more accurately, the cause of the fear is the inability of the self to feel supported by its selfobjects and to be uplifted by its values and understandings. Look for self issues when death issues arise.

ST. L'S WORSHIP

There are new, often unexpected challenges to our self cohesion as we age. Those capacities and appearances that once elicited mirroring responses of praise and admiration fade away. Relied upon idealized figures die. Familiar neighborhoods and family surroundings once providing alterego assurances of belonging, are lost as one enters strange care facilities.

Perhaps there is no more crucial time to remember these self realities than when the pastor visits a nursing home. First, those in care facilities continue to need reassurance that they are connected. That human yearning does not diminish as one ages. Touches that connect are as life-essential in later stages as the mother's touch is in giving psychological birth to her little child.

For example, an aged pastor was confined to nursing home care. Parkinson's disease had silenced his voice and clouded his mind. On frequent occasions at the home, an elderly woman, who was disoriented and not responsible for her actions, would begin shrieking and screaming hysterically, with sedation the only effective intervention. To these turbulent outbursts the other residents would react with angry complaints, yelling at her to shut up. One day the enfeebled pastor was sitting next to her as she began her ritual wailing. After a few moments, his worn hand reached out and touched her gently on the arm—the way it had on countless other arms in his ministry before, now perhaps enabled by some breakthrough in his own clouded consciousness, perhaps only as an instinctual pastoral response—and the disturbed woman became quiet and peaceful. This woman was calmed through the presence of a human touch, through a humanizing touch, which conveyed in a primitive, beyond-words-way that she was connected to humanity, linked with another human being who resonated with her anguish. She was not alone, for there was another of essential likeness near her. Active pastors visiting nursing care centers can facilitate responses that restore assurances of being connected.

Second, as one grows old, one still relies upon adequately abundant, sufficiently stimulating, and reasonably accurate selfobject responses. At this time these responses may be even more critical than when a person was more emotionally and cognitively robust.

At a convalescent home a nurse wheeled an elderly woman away from the front of the elevator. The nurse said, "You know you're not suppose to be by the elevator." There was no discernable reply from the woman, but one could gather what the elderly lady must have said to the nurse because the nurse then said, "Well, one of us is not telling the truth." On a deep level one can imagine that the elderly woman was indeed "telling the truth": the truth of her right to be there, the truth of her lingering sense of freedom, the truth of her ongoing, authentic validation of her self when she must have said, "Yes I can." The nurse was responding to the truth as adherence to rules. The woman was responding to the truth of what was rightfully her self's truth. It would have been better if the nurse, with empathic understanding, had said something more mirror-affirming, like, "You are very good at wheeling your self all around here, and I'm glad you can, but the elevator can be a dangerous place. That's why we ask people to stay clear of it." A pastor's understanding of what brings relief is as important as understanding what brings grief.

When pastors preach at nursing homes, whatever message they intend to deliver can be crafted with empathic selfobject undertones in mind. The following short mediation was delivered during Advent.

> We have a Christmas clock in our kitchen that plays a brief version of a holiday carol on the hour—if there is enough light. When there is sufficient light a light sensor is set off and the clock plays a tune. When there isn't sufficient light the clock plays nothing.
>
> Now some people are kind of like that: when they get light, sun light, they run pretty good. But when the light is short, like in winter or when days are cloudy, then the lack of sun makes them listless, gloomy, irritable. They don't run well, and they certainly don't make beautiful music. This is called the SAD syndrome: the "Seasonal Affective Disorder" syndrome.
>
> But there are people who are more persistently like this. Unless there is some spotlight shinning on them, something that continually makes them feel special or continually entertains them or continually seems exciting, they become bored, gloomy, and irritable.
>
> What really impresses me are people who can sing in the dark, sing when the light is gone or blocked out and the only light they have is the one in their mind or heart—a remembered light, a hoped for light, even an imagined light that keeps them running, keeps them singing. These people inspire me, probably because I worry that if the light stops shinning then I, too, will fall into a gloomy mood.
>
> I often ask older people at funerals if coming to funerals is hard for them because it might remind them of their own death. It's been encouraging to me to find that most people have made some peace with their own dying, that as the light begins to fade around them and within them, they still keep running, still keep embracing life as much as they can. They don't sit on the sideline watching life go by and waiting, waiting for the bus of death to come pick them up. And so I say to you and to myself, "Keep the light glowing inside you." You are blessed when you do, and a blessing to others as well.

These words were intended to inform and encourage the selves of elderly residents. Throughout were descriptions of self fragmentation and why that happens. Mirroring affirmations were given by the pastor for those who could keep singing in the dark. Alterego responses were offered by the pastor by connecting his own vulnerability to gloominess to that of others. Idealized figures were lifted up as sources of inspiration as the pastor identified calm, collected individual who lived their closing days with peace. What carries any pastoral message is the empathic envelope in which is it delivered.

VISIT WITH DISABLED/RETIRING COLLEAGUE

Rev S called his visit with a colleague who was disabled/retired and moving away a "pastoral visit." Whether the colleague expected Rev S to function in some pastoral capacity or whether Rev S simply considered all such visits "pastoral" we do not know. But it is important that Rev S know. Pastors need clarity about what may be expected of them in certain situations, or at least need to be prepared for what might be expected of them. Part of the implicit and explicit expectations people have of their selfobjects is that they will enact appropriate roles at appropriate times. When selfobject figures fail to carry out their assigned roles, then some form of narcissistic rage and/or depletion typically arises.

The disabled/retired/moving colleague may not need Rev S to function as a pastor. While he may not strongly object if Rev S does so, in his heart he may not be reaching out for Rev S's "pastoral presence" or his words of faith. Instead, the colleague may look for Rev S to be just that—a colleague, with whom he can enjoy alterego conversation and musings before he moves to where he has doubts of finding such self-same connections. Or, the person may inwardly desire for Rev S to come simply as a friend, who will remember him in his former glory days of bodily strength and productive employment and applaud who he was—if not still is. Or perhaps the person does want Rev S to enact the role of pastor, as one who is willing to enter into the atmosphere of the person's disrupted body, work, and home and offer spirit-calming words of hope.

Rev. S is a skillful pastor who has the ability to enact various self-object roles, functioning as pastor at one moment, colleague at the next, and friend at another. Or more accurately stated, in pastoral relationships he can be a "friend-inclined pastor," a "colleague-inclined pastor," or a "pastor-inclined pastor." Deciding which role should be the lead role in certain circumstances is vital, however, for the healing of injured selves.

Pastors are helpful at times when they clearly signal to others what role they are determined to be in and stay in, such as when a male pastor calls upon a single young woman who has recently lost her mother. Staying "the pastor" sets helpful boundaries on pastor and parishioner alike. Moreover, pastors can legitimately consider themselves as doing everything "from a pastoral heart," meaning that at all times they try to be channels of God's grace. Here being pastoral is more than a job description; it is a way of being in the world. But it is not helpful when pastors constantly "put on their pastor face," or meet every situation with ministerial overtones, if not with overt language and gesture.

Clergy function best when they are able to be empathically flexible, which means being able to discern the selfobject role most needed by persons in states of stress and to respond accordingly. This doesn't mean trying to be all things to all people, or losing one's identity by constantly molding one's self to the expectations of others. Instead, it lifts up the validity of allowing one's self to accommodate to the selfobject needs of others, especially when their hold on life and limb is weakened. What all of us have to offer each other at the very depth of our life together is our willingness to serve as an adequate selfobject figure. That requires empathic flexibility.

That is not always easy. Providing adequate selfobject support requires the giver to have at least an adequate state of self cohesion and self-esteem. Being a selfobject can be rewarding; it can also be draining. Moreover, it is not always clear from the outset what is needed in certain circumstances, and so pastors often fumble. "I was admiring when I needed to be inspiring, and I tried to be inspiring when I needed to be revealing," lamented one self psychology–informed minister. What he meant was that he was offering mirroring responses when the person needed him to be a source of uplifting idealized feelings and thoughts, yet in another situation where he tried to enact the role of idealized provider of uplifting feelings and thoughts the group needed him to stand revealed in their midst as one of them, as a participating alterego. Using the self psychology template gets easier with practice, however.

Kohut's perspective might help Rev S with another aspect of his "pastoral call" upon his colleague: the person's disability. Kohut often talks about the "body-mind self," by which he means that the body and its functions and the mind and its functions are simultaneously the primary representations of the self. At times Kohut turns "body-mind self" (without the hyphen) into self terminology by hyphenating body-mind with self, resulting in "body-mind-self." In any case, "body-mind self" and "body-mind-self" are the same.

Terminology clarifications are important here for two reasons. First, Kohut is not unique in suggesting that the elemental dimensions of a person's being are the body and the mind. That is commonly agreed upon. However, and second, "body-mind self" and especially "body-mind-self" might cause a reader to assume that Kohut means that the body and its functions and the mind and its functions constitute the self, "make up" the self—which is also a common assumption. That is not what Kohut means. What sets Kohut apart, as we have seen in previous chapters, is the way he takes what is (like Freud's drives) and incorporates it into a new framework, namely into an understanding about the "self." Similarly here, Kohut redefines the nature of body and mind. They are not autonomous; nor are body and mind and self equal domains. The body and its functions and the mind and its functions are parts of the self. These parts do not build up the self; they become built into the self. It is the self that incorporates and brings into smooth functioning the developing capacities of the body and mind. Body and mind, and their functions, therefore, have "narcissistic meaning" as it were; that is, they are parts of the self, infused agents of the self's mirroring, idealizing and alterego strivings, and immediate indicators of the self's diminished self cohesion and self-esteem.

This means that the disability of Rev S's colleague is more than and deeper than a medical issue, or family issue, or financial issue. It is a self issue. The very core of the colleague's self is centrally involved. What is injured is more than the body; the self has been injured. All the mirroring, idealizing, alterego yearnings and values and hopes and dreams surrounding the body have been shaken to some degree. Nothing has been left untouched.

There's a more clinical way to put this. A person responds to their own body as their selfobject. Indeed, Kohut uses the example of how we expect our arm to rise when we want it to rise and how we become angry or despondent when it does not do our bidding as an illustration of how in general we relate to others as selfobjects and expect them to function. Our body is our selfobject. Not only do we expect it to do our bidding, we rely upon it for narcissistic well-being. For example, how one looks, how fast one can run, and how long one can survive in the backwoods can all become body-based sources of self-esteem and established foundations for one's inner sense of having secure cohesion: feeling strong, balanced, resilient. When those capacities fade, or are no more, angry reactions may surface. Tendencies to want to hide, to withdraw from the world, may happen. The person might regress to a near preoccupation with the body and its processes. When disabled people become preoccupied with bowel functions, for example, this may signal not just physiological change but also psychological fragmentation. Life shrinks from feeling bodily whole to near exclusive focus on a single body function. Intense concern for a single body function is also, however, the person's desperate attempt to protect their physical intactness and overcome fears of "coming unglued." Rev S's empathic sensitivities could be broadened by grasping these self-understandings.

Rev S might be helped with one more realization. The body is not the self, although what happens to the body greatly affects the self's cohesion and esteem. That means that the self can rise above whatever happens to the body. And this we often, and joyfully, see.

At a hastily called meeting, a woman who had just found out she had breast cancer cried out, "My body has betrayed me!" Her shocked pastor regained his composure and began the long process of helping her hold herself together—physically and mentally. It was difficult for her. There were setbacks, uncertainty, and finally the discovery that she would never recover, even after surgery.

But she did not disintegrate. Loving family members, supportive friends, potluck-bringing parishioners, an available and understanding pastor, and a God who was never too far from her helped her maintain her equilibrium. And so she declared in the last months of her life, "My body is worse, but my spirit is better." The body may move decisively toward death, but one's spirit can still survive, can still look up at the light from cherished values and sing.

CATCHING UP WITH T

"Spouses are parishioners, too!" exclaimed the wife of a busy minister. This was more than an attempt to carve out time with him by saying something like, "Just treat me as one of your church members. Then I might at least have some of your undivided attention." Yes, it was this, but more. It was her yearning to have a pastor in her life, to have an ordained figure, a "set-apart" person of God in her life whose sermons could uplift her, whose affirmations of her faith could give her quiet joy, and whose efforts to create an atmosphere of acceptance in the church could help her feel she belonged.

Pastors let slip from their mind the reality that spouses are often parishioners, with the same selfobject needs from the pastor as other parishioners. What typically happens is that pastors rely upon the support of their selfobject spouse to keep their self cohesive enough to do their pastoral work. Indeed, pastors may turn to their spouse even more intensely for those selfobject responses that are not coming from the parish. The spouse becomes the target for the fragmenting pastor's yearning/demand for mirroring, idealizing or alterego responses that have been thwarted by the congregation.

Struggling pastors have a hard enough time being a spouse to their spouse let alone being also a pastor to their spouse. The answer is not to make the spouse a co-worker in the church or a "behind-the-scenes co-pastor." That may generate more time between them but it may still leave the spouse feeling pastor-less.

This is not the place for a fuller discussion of how pastors can minister to their wives or husbands. Some simple suggestions must suffice. For example, pastors at home can lead devotions, lead discussion of what scriptural texts might mean for the family, and lead in prayer. The minister might resist reading the Sunday sermon to the spouse, avoid going over it with the spouse for clarity of ideas or correctness of tone. Instead the spouse might be granted the opportunity to hear the word afresh, to feel at one with the congregation who listens attentively for what emerges next. Finally, pastors might also curtail overwhelming discussion with the spouse about the inner workings of the church that bring the pastor great headaches if not heartaches. Just as clergy try to generate a spirit of hope in the church even when things are difficult, so can the pastor do that with the spouse/parishioner.

It may also be hard for pastors to minister to their spouses for an opposite reason: spouses may yearn for the presence of a pastor yet be unable to respond to their spouse as a pastor. One spouse said she could get nothing out of the sermons her husband preached because for her it was "just my husband talking." Other spouses find it hard to experience any idealization attachment to their pastor/spouse because they "know what is done behind closed doors. You see one person; I know the

person beneath that." Then again, spouses may not benefit from a pas-
tor/spouse's affirming statements because "I've heard you use that same
tone of voice and same words in church meetings. It seems artificial here
between us, put on."

For spouses who can't experience their pastor/spouse as a pastor,
it may be necessary for the spouse to connect with other pastors on the
staff, if there are such pastors, or to find spiritual comfort by connecting with inspiring parishioners whose grace and wisdom nourish the
spouse's soul. If all else fails, a spouse may need to attend another church
to find the pastoral presence so desired. Churches are far more receptive
to this arrangement than they have been in the past. That is, they are
less inclined to experience this non-attendance as an act of rejection,
a narcissistic injury. Finally, it would be hoped that pastor and spouse
might become familiar with the self psychology dynamics that happen
between people and let these new explanations slip into the privacy of
the clergy couple's bedroom.

FROM MEDITATION TO BEATING OF DRUMS

There is one other person Rev S took good care of that busy Sunday—
himself. Pastors need to pastor their own self, and Rev S did. In a variety
of ways he recharged his self through selfobject involvements.

He attempted to strengthen and restored his self through idealizing
mergers. First was his early morning meditation where he let himself
be lifted up into the power of God's presence. Second was his attempt
to vicariously share the glory of his idealized selfobject Yankees, only to
find, alas, that their failure added to his self's deflation (a mild case of
narcissistic depletion).

Rev S also engaged in mirror-affirming activities to shore up his self.
One was his playing of the drums, which not only gave him invigorating
pleasure but also served to reaffirm for him that, yes, indeed, he did possess outstanding musical talent. Another was his complete reading of the
New York Times (sans the magazine section), which not only gave him a
reassuring sense of "being in the know," but also reaffirmed for him that,
yes, indeed, he also possessed outstanding intellectual ability.

Finally, Rev S at the last attempted to infuse his tired self with a
soothing glow by reaching out for alterego contact with an old friend as
he drowsily sent a late evening email. And now he could go to bed, having worked hard, having been drained to some degree by all his pastoral

encounters, but now restored to a reasonable state of well-being. His self was firm, awaiting another day with relaxed anticipation.

There is a strange paradox, however, between having a firm self and being vulnerable to fragmentation of the self. It is wonderful, for example, when pastors can have enough self-esteem and self cohesion that they are "open" to the world. Here they can come out from behind their defenses that try to protect their mirror-sensitive, idealization-sensitive, or alterego-sensitive selves. Here they can wade into life without undue apprehension about suffering a narcissistic injury. They can embrace the world with broad empathy.

But the more a person, like a pastor, is open to the world via a firm self, the more one is also open to the great sadness in the world, to the unremedial nature of much of life, to the inevitable and consistent ways in which people are unconcerned for if not cruel to others. These can wear thin the spirit of even the most secure individual.

But there is more. The stronger the self of the pastor is, the more people are inclined to attach themselves to the pastor, to expect the pastor to function for them as a sacrificing selfobject. Needy parishioners suck nourishment from strong pastors, not because they are jealous of them but because the apparently strong pastor has narcissistic sustenance that depleted individuals or groups so desperately yearn for. This happened to Jesus on several occasions. He was nearly sucked dry by the clamoring needs of the crowds who made him their life-sustaining selfobject, so much so that he needed to withdraw before his depleted self gave way to more severe forms of narcissistic rage than his irritable demand to "Heal yourself!"

The problem with clergy is that they aren't always as skillful as Jesus at taking a break. They are on average moderate to poor in self-care. The more people demand of them, the more they may slip into an archaic grandiosity where they think they really are special and people can't get along without them. Or, they may slip into anxious feelings that if they take time out for themselves, others will be critical of them for being self-centered, or for not doing a good enough job. The problems pastors have with maintaining healthy self-care activities are primarily narcissistic problems, not time management problems. Beneath each complaint by a pastor that he or she doesn't have enough time for self-care is a self who is vulnerable to being injured by the congregation. One pastor said, "I'm motivated not so much by the thought of winning as I am by the fear of failing, by the fear of being criticized." Good self-care begins with an em-pathic understanding of one's narcissistic strivings and vulnerabilities.

CONCLUSION

Our profession as pastors is to love. The only qualifying feature is to love wisely. Unconditional love is never possible and is sometimes blind in its attempts. Kohut's self psychology perspective helps pastors love wisely. That doesn't mean that understanding the self will always keep us from pain, or from making mistakes, or from wanting to give up. But it does help us be wise enough to hold on, to live for another day, with the hope and the knowledge that thankfully our self cohesion can be restored and that supportive selfobject responses often come from the most unexpected of places. Hang in there. The nature of the self is to regain equilibrium.

END NOTES

1.   Discussed in Homans, *Ability to Mourn*, 45–46.

5

Pastoral Care of the Church as a Group Self

A MINISTER TELLS OF being dissuaded in seminary from writing a dissertation on "personalities of parishes." "You can't apply individual psychology to complex, heterogeneous groups," warned his sociologically minded teacher. Methodology aside for the moment, just ask any seasoned minister, denominational leader, or pastoral consultant if congregations have distinct "personalities" and you will see faces light up—or grimace—in affirmation.

Self psychology supports this general impression. One of Kohut's important contributions was to show how a group can be understood to function as a "self" analogous to the self of an individual. The self of a group is its inner psychological core around which it is organized and from which it acts and experiences itself. Being a group, each church functions as a self. From a self psychology perspective, therefore, a church's self, like an individual's self, endeavors to live a full and productive life by attaching to empathic selfobject figures who provide mirroring, idealizing, and alterego responses. Furthermore, the church as a self also strives to maintain a firm sense of self cohesion, which the self experiences as having positive and reliable self-esteem, being whole and harmonious, zestful and invigorated, and possessing a sense of sameness over time, of having continuity and firm identity. Finally, the church's self, like the self of an individual, inevitably experiences narcissistic injuries—blows to the self's aims and expectations—and responds in mature or regressive ways to restore its fragmented self cohesion. Kohut's self psychology perspective helps us see that each church can be understood as a self who is psychologically animated by its efforts to satisfy its narcissistic strivings, find supportive selfobject figures, and protect, maintain, and restore its self cohesion.

To say that a church "has" a self erroneously suggests that the self is subordinate to something higher, or grounded in something more fundamental. The church's "personality," for example, or its "identity," is not the foundation for its "self." Instead, the "self" is the foundation for its personality and identity. Likewise, to say that a church "is" a self erroneously suggests an equation between the terms "church" and "self." The church self does not worship; it does not intentionally move in the world preaching, teaching, and serving. Instead, the church as a living community of believers does this, acting with deliberation and will. It is more accurate, therefore, to say that a church "functions" as a self. The "self" of the church is its bedrock psychological structure by which it functions in particular ways in the world. The narcissistic character of a church's self shapes how the church carries out its purposes, ideals, and actions. It determines levels of striving and productivity. It facilitates, or impedes, the establishment of supportive relationships human and divine.

Pastoral care of the church as a group self can begin by observing and attempting to understand the inner, subjective experiences of the church's self. That is, the self psychology–informed caregiver directs attention to the church's core self needs, its selfobject yearnings, and the narcissistic injuries it has experienced, along with the impact of these injuries on its self cohesion. In the first section of this chapter, we move back and forth between empathic observations of one particular parish, St M, and empathic conceptions regarding the needs of its self. In doing so, we will be highlighting structures of the group self common to all parishes. In the second section of this chapter we will delineate particular needs of church selves based upon the level of their self cohesion, suggesting how best to empathically respond.

There are two more prefacing remarks that need to be made. First, this chapter can be used in several ways. It explicitly provides a self psychology orientation for those whose designated pastoral function is to provide interventions, counseling, or consultation with struggling churches. It can be used in a wider way by those who are interested in learning more about Kohut's concept of group self and how it might be clinically described. This chapter can also be used by psychologically minded parishioners who desire to understand more completely the church they so dearly love. Finally, this chapter's not-so-subtle message is also for narcissistically injured clergy who are simply reaching for whatever resource they can find to hold their self together.

Second, all of the clinical cases throughout this chapter have been altered or merged with other cases to provide confidentiality. This is more than just a legal matter; it ultimately is part of what it means to be an empathically responding selfobject.

OBSERVING AND UNDERSTANDING THE CHURCH'S SELF

The clerk of session from St M called for an emergency meeting with a denominational leader whose pastoral care ministry provided interventions for struggling churches. "We're falling apart," the clerk exclaimed. "A large number of parishioners call Rev E a 'devil' who is destroying our congregation. A vocal minority support him and his work. Each faction is at the other's throat. The life of the church has dwindled down to nothing more than preoccupation with this issue. We've got to do something."

Shortly afterwards the denominational leader received a call from a livid Rev E. They had gone too far! It had been all he could do to restrain his anger at the criticisms he publicly received from disgruntled members, but now they had said things to his wife that left her terribly shaken. He couldn't wait to confront them, to unleash on them the fury he had inside. As a result of all this he wasn't sleeping well, his chest was continuously tight and aching, and he could not concentrate on his work. Something had to be done.

Later accounts of the church's story revealed to the denominational leader that St M had been an old rural congregation basically made up of members raised in the church, many whose fathers and mothers had literally built the church nail by plank. These parishioners had a deep affinity for the building, for parish life, and for one another. Worship, programs, and social activities were shaped around the needs and themes of rural life familiar to and participated in by all. The church even expected its pastor to be like them, to the point where he was directed to wear jeans and a flannel shirt as his daily garb, rather than a business suit, which would set him apart.

Rapid industrial development in the area resulted in unexpected growth for St. M. Within a few years, new individuals joined the church and became vocal members. These persons brought not only new dollars but also new expectations. The comfortable, familiar atmosphere began to change, as did the type of programs offered. Pastoral leadership shifted as well, as Rev E, with strong administrative abilities, was called to serve as their new minister. A large segment of the church eventually found its ways of doing things invaded and violated by "those people." Intense conflicts arose between old family parishioners and those who saw themselves as the new wave.

Rev E became the focal point of this controversy. Old parishioners complained of not feeling comfortable in his presence, of his business-like demeanor and his to-the-point attitude in worship and visitations. He himself felt that he had been given a mandate by the parish to "put this church on the map." Such a project personally suited him as he enjoyed directing church life and being in the public eye.

St M had been struggling with its own internal injuries prior to the cultural invasion of the new wave and the new minister. Their beloved, down-home pastor—whose declared ecclesiastical style was that of "friendship ministry"—had traumatized the church by having an affair with one of its members. They continued to care for him but felt compelled to ask him to leave. No one talked much about it. For several long months they were in limbo, being served off and on by various interim clergy.

Rev. E also came to St M with freshly sustained injuries. He felt his previous congregation had not appreciated him. He saw his role as that of leader, but that former church had not followed his directions. In order not to jeopardize his position, he refrained from public expressions of his rage. His wife, however, became the vehicle by which his complaints and grievances were known to the parish. Rev E came to St M expecting a new beginning.

The denominational leader had some familiarity with the self psychology perspective and let it inform his observations and understandings. He sensed that St M from the start had not been a loose collection of diverse individuals. There had been cohesion in this multiplicity of persons, a sense of continuity and sameness through time, and a particular way in which they had been bonded together. For the denominational leader this was understood as the "self" of that original parish; that which gave psychological structure and form to St M as an institutional gathering of parishioners over time had been the group's self. It was to the nature and vicissitudes of this group self that the denominational leader directed his observations and understanding.

We have indicated previously that there are three central features of the church's self that can inform pastoral care observation and understanding: the nature of its narcissistic aims; the character of its selfobject relationships; and the quality of its self cohesion. While part and parcel of each other, we discuss them separately for deeper clarity.

Narcissistic Aims

Empathic observation of church life generally indicates that the self of a congregation, like the self of an individual, congeals around a particular narcissistic orientation (self need). Some churches have strong self needs for what Kohut calls "mirroring." They need to experience others affirming, applauding, or complimenting them for their specialness and for what they do. When this happens, they are able to maintain feelings of positive self-esteem, to experience assured feelings of harmony, strength, and zest, and to adequately restore a sense of well-being when their mirroring needs are thwarted and their self cohesion is fragmented to some degree. Other churches have strong self needs for what Kohut calls "idealizing." They need to experience being a part of, or to merge with, inspiring and admired others, to share in their charisma and power. When this happens on a dependable basis, the church is able to maintain feelings of inner security and calmness, to care for others with the same uplifting spirit they have experienced, and to restore their fragmented self cohesion when narcissistically wounded. Finally, other churches have strong self needs for "alterego responses." They need to experience others as being like them in a variety of ways, or identical to them in crucial ways. When this happens on a consistent basis, this provides the church with an assurance of being bonded and of belonging. It sustains their feelings of human connectedness and inner identity, along with a feeling of firmness in body, mind, and spirit, thus allowing them to adequately regulate their fragmenting tensions when suffering blows to their self-expectations. While each church expresses all three of these narcissistic strivings, one narcissistic aim (self need) tends to emerge dominant, giving the church its particular character.

The denominational leader came to understand that St M as a rural parish was formed originally around the need to express and enhance its alterego relating. Mirroring needs did not appear prevalent, nor were there strong yearnings for the presence of idealized figures. The influx of persons who did not share the history and attitudes of this alterego group self failed to function in similar alterego ways, failed to function as alterego selfobjects, and thus threatened the rural church's psychological core.

As the church's self cohesion began to fragment, great expressions of anger arose. Kohut uses the term "narcissistic rage" for the wide range of angry responses that arise when an individual's or group's selfobjects fail to act in the way they are expected to act. He uses the term "narcissistic withdrawal" for the wide range of depressive reactions that might also arise when one is extremely disappointed in the actions of one's cherished selfobject figures. In the case of St M, xenophobic language, demonic images, and uncivil behaviors arose in the wake of narcissistic rage as the original contingent fought to reinstate the primacy of their alterego aims and programs.

A congregation striving to fulfill its primary self-aim may be able to move to a reliance upon a compensating self-aim when that primary aim is thwarted. For instance, a church motivated by strong mirroring needs was forced to face the embarrassment of public ridicule and denominational intervention when its grandly acclaimed pastor was caught shoplifting. In an effort to soothe itself and to regain its self cohesion, the church withdrew into an idealizing merger with God. The psychological boundaries of the church's self momentarily shrank to where it turned intensely inward, giving itself overwhelmingly to worship and prayer and to hyper-attentive efforts to decipher signs of God's direction for them. Such compensating self-aims can influence the church's future style and goals. Typically, however, a church will revert to its primary self-aim when its narcissistic equilibrium (self cohesion) is restored.

Selfobject Relationships

The fulfillment of a church's self-aims (for mirroring, idealizing, or alterego relating) requires the sustaining presence of empathically responding selfobject figures. Selfobjects, once again, are individuals, groups, things, ideas, or anything that a self takes as part of its self, as an extension of its self (hence the term "selfobject"), which the self implicitly expects, and often explicitly demands, to act in mirroring, idealizing, or alterego ways. For Kohut, the life-giving milieu of selfobject responses to the individual's or group's self needs constitute the very foundation of all psychological life. At work psychologically, therefore, in the formation, maintenance, and repair of the church self is the mobilization and use of vital selfobject figures.

The parish pastor is typically the primary selfobject figure affecting the church's self-esteem and self cohesion. Certain parishioners may be selfobject figures for the congregations, as may revered denominational officials. But the current pastor or pastors carry the weight of selfobject expectations.

Within church life, however, not only does the self of the church expect the pastor to be its selfobject (thus forming a self-selfobject relationship with the pastor), but the church simultaneously becomes a selfobject for the self of the pastor (who forms his or her own self-selfobject relationship with the parish). The pastor expects the parish to respond in empathic, responsive ways to the pastor's own mirroring, idealizing, or alterego needs. As a consequence, a pastor may react with some form of narcissistic rage and/or depressive withdrawal when the church fails to provide the required selfobject responses that the pastor needs for the protection and enhancement of the pastor's own esteem and cohesion. Similarly, the church as a group self may (and often does) respond with rage and/or depressive withdrawal when its selfobject pastor responds in less than ideal ways. In short, the primary selfobject relationship in the church is the one formed between the parish as a group self and the pastor as an individual self, in which each expects the other to function in particular selfobject ways.

In the past, St M had been served by pastors who reflected the essential sameness of its members. As alterego selfobjects, they were expected to preserve and enhance the alterego alliances and agendas of the church's self. Rev E came to St M with strong mirroring needs. When he was injured by non-responsiveness or outright criticism, he began to fragment (lose self cohesion) and required even more intense mirroring responses to keep himself together. Such healing grace, however, did not appear often enough or powerfully enough.

Although the old guard parishioners now opposed Rev E, as a group they had joined newer members in calling him as their pastor. From listening with a self psychology ear, the denominational leader began to understand the narcissistic motivations for this action. The affair of their beloved alterego pastor had been devastating to St M. As a result, the church was left with hidden anger over his failure, grief over losing him, and hypersensitivity to being served by a pastor who might again be "weak and vulnerable." The old guard momentarily moved to an idealizing selfobject relationship with Rev E, whose strength and professed self-certainty they could merge with in order to restore their shaken self-esteem and self cohesion. His espoused power promised safety from human dalliance, and provided soothing detraction from their grief—at least for a time. His ultimate selfobject function, therefore, was not really to "put them on the map" but instead to restore the old map, to return them to their former alterego state of well-being. All this, of course, was internally at work and only dimly, if at all, in the awareness of the alterego-minded parishioners.

Unfortunately Rev E could not and did not fulfill the parish's implicit selfobject expectations, due mainly to the contrary demands of his own selfobject expectations for the church. As often happens when interviewing pastoral candidates, a church's urgent self needs blunt its observational capacities for distinguishing between optimally suited selfobject candidates and those whose external language and behavior conceal different narcissistic agendas. Similarly, narcissistically wounded pastors are inclined to cognitively distort what they hear and understand about the church's potential for restoring the pastors' own damaged self. It is not that churches and pastors are routinely dishonest with each other; it's more that they are not adequately informed about the nature and power of selfobject needs and the impacts on body, mind, and spirit when self cohesion is fragile. The psychological core of most ecclesiastical conflict is composed of the clash between the cardinal selfobject needs of the church's self and the dominant selfobject need of the pastor's self.

Regulation of Self Cohesion

A crucial feature of a church's self is the development of reliable, self-regulating capacities necessary for maintaining and restoring self cohesion. Among these self-regulating functions are: the capacity to integrate drives and impulses into a smoothly coordinated whole; the capacity for reality testing and participant observation; the capacity to respond empathically to others and to the church's own self; the capacity to be lead and uplifted by the church's ideals, values, and goals; the capacity to maintain positive self-esteem in the face of criticisms or separations from selfobject figures rather than react with regressive expressions of rage and/or withdraw; and the capacity to make appropriate use of selfobject figures. Pastoral care of the parish self entails assessing the strengths and deficiencies of its self-regulatory functions, and consequently the reliability or unreliability of its self cohesion.

It seemed clear to the denominational leader that the selves of St M and Rev E were in a state of severe fragmentation. They were unable to maintain their own self-esteem and self cohesion in the face of narcissistic injuries they experienced. The capacity for self-soothing was lost, as evidenced in the expressions of intense narcissistic rage (parishioners' wide-ranging efforts to hurt anything attached to the pastor; the pastor's press for revenge). The ability to self-observe and to employ reality testing was diminished, as shown in the rise of disturbed and regressive thought processes (the church's paranoid-like beliefs that the pastor was a devil and its obsessive preoccupations with being done wrong; the pastor's loss of smooth mental functioning). Both parish and pastor were also unable to maintain a sense of bodily wholeness (the schism in the church; the pastor's physical disturbances). And both demonstrated eroded capacities for empathy, creativity, and hope. In summary, they were unable to feel good about themselves and be led by their higher values. They were unable to remain calm, analytical, and open to inspiration. They were unable to experience any sense of belonging with opposite others or any sense that in spite of differences they were essentially all the same.

HEALING RESPONSES TO FRAGMENTED PARISHES

We now describe three broad types of parish selves whose self-cohesion has been shaken. These types of fragmentation could also be used to understand struggling pastors as well. Within each type we also suggest the central healing need for that injured church, along with suggestions for the optimal therapeutic response by the pastoral caregivers in the position to be channels of grace. In the type of parish disorder called "disintegrating parish selves" we present a more thorough account of how the self psychology perspective can inform assessments about the level of a church's lost cohesion and can shape concrete interventions. Getting a feel for a self psychology approach to this particular parish disorder will allow a briefer analysis of the two remaining types.

In spite of clear differences between types of lost self cohesion, there is a great deal of overlap. Parishes, like individuals, are seldom just this way or that. As Kohut has repeatedly noted, there are constant "vacillations" in self structure. Correspondingly, the caregiver may also find the usefulness of blending some of the approaches we offer for each type of fragmented parish. What we present are orienting guidelines informed by our work in the healing perspective of Kohut's self psychology.

Disintegrating Parish Selves

The selves of some parishes are in a state of escalating fragmentation. Kohut uses the term "disintegration" to describe the self cohesion of individuals and groups that were severely falling apart and in danger of complete collapse. Disintegrating selves may have started out chronically weak and defectively structured from their beginning and are thus exceptionally vulnerable to severe forms of fragmentation. Other disintegrating churches may have regressed to this condition from previous states of firm self cohesion. In both situations, however, the parish is in crisis.

Disintegrating self cohesion may occur when church selves are traumatized by highly regarded selfobject figures who suddenly withdraw, act in grossly disturbing ways, or "side with the enemy," for example. Then again, disintegration may also stem from the church's inadequate self-regulating resources for self-soothing, for empathic understanding, or for making use of other available selfobjects, for example. These and other self-regulation resources tend to be enfeebled in disintegrating congregations. Consequently, such churches are unable to compensate for weakness in one self resource by using the strength of a different self resource.

As indicated, it appeared that St M and Rev E were experiencing severe fragmentation. Because the selves of the pastor and the parish were vulnerable to escalating expressions of narcissistic rage and/or depressive withdrawal in the face of increasing tensions, the denominational leader decided to meet with the pastor and the session separately at first. The session was psychologically disordered enough without having the pastor present as an igniting lightning rod. Similarly, it was best not to provide a sitting target for Rev. E's intense level of narcissistic rage. Protecting what remnant of self cohesion might still exist for St M and Rev E was mandatory. The denominational leader's self psychology assessment was that an initial face-to- face meeting would exacerbate tensions, on the one hand, and not allow him to devote undivided, empathic attentiveness to injured selves, on the other.

Self psychology assessments regarding prevailing states of self cohesion and the potential for further fragmentation are crucial data when considering arrangements mandated by other therapeutic approaches. For example, a family therapy model might require that all participants in the conflict be present in order to effectively change the system of relationships. A theological model might call for restoration via a whole-church approach, where confrontation, confession, and forgiveness are the means for renewed community. These arrangements could be efficacious in circumstances where signs of continued selfobject support exist between minister and congregation, along with evidence of residual capacities for self-regulation of tensions and for making empathic responses. From a self psychology perspective, the prevailing cohesion of selves is a cardinal criteria by which the use of other arrangement strategies or therapeutic approaches is considered for particular situations.

When working with a disintegrating parish self, the approach that brings the most immediate healing grace is where a pastoral caregiver takes the role of "substituting selfobject," as we term it. That is, the caregiver provides structure and direction for parish life, stands in for absent mirroring, idealizing, or alterego figures the parish and pastor so desperately need, and in essential ways substitutes for those missing self functions that the self of parish is presently (or chronically) unable to enact for its self. Action is called for. The caregiver operates in concrete, deliberate ways in an effort to "put on the brakes," to stop the downward spiral of church's disintegrating self cohesion.

As a substitute for the parish's limited or missing capacities for maintaining self cohesion, the in-action caregiver manages critical affairs. For instance, the denominational leader strongly suggested to St M that a quickly arranged congregational meeting to vote on whether Rev E should go or stay should not happen. Certainly the church needed to "do something" to ease the incredible tension it was experiencing, the denominational leader empathically expressed, but the proposed solution via voting would very likely incite more hurt and anger than it would remove.

Inasmuch as a disintegrating parish also tends to be highly sensitive to criticism, moral injunctions or biblical judgments are contraindicated except in rare situations. A self psychology informed pastoral caregiver may decide that confronting the parish with powerful moral or biblical dictates is the only way to stop further deterioration of its nuclear core. Typically, however, imposing psychological or theo-ethical mandates upon a fragmenting self deplete in self-esteem is often experienced as just another injury.

Fragmented selves are receptive, even desperate at times, for newly involved selfobject figures. That is why a newly involved caregiver can function from the beginning in the mode of substituting selfobject. St M and Rev E implicitly called upon the denominational leader to fulfill this substituting selfobject role when they urgently requested/demanded that he "do something." It is common for fragmenting, panic-stricken individuals and groups to want someone to powerfully enter in and "do something" for them, to do anything that will alleviate the overwhelming feeling of falling apart. The pastoral caregiver who utilizes this approach attempts to function as a "doing" selfobject for the church whose cohesion is in meltdown mode.

Whatever structural "doing" might be necessary is preceded, however, by a "doing" function that is always first and foremost no matter what level of lost self cohesion a church may suffer: providing an empathic atmosphere in which church members feel understood. This subjective experience of someone listening attentively and sensing deeply what the group or individual experiences is the bedrock of all other restorative efforts. It is the first and necessary infusion of healing grace for injured selves.

Awareness of this crucial doing function of empathic listening and understanding also shaped the denominational leader's decision to meet separately at first with session members and the pastor. A common approach when pastor-parish conflicts arise is to declare, "The first thing to do is to get the pastor and congregation together and help them understand themselves and understand each other." Such a point of departure would have been therapeutically inadvisable from a self psychology perspective. Instead, what St M and Rev E first needed was to feel understood. Kohut helps us comprehend more completely that giving injured others the feeling of being understood is the first and often primary healing response we offer as empathically responding selfobjects. It was this understanding milieu that the denominational leader intended to supply in his opening meetings, which could be established more readily and consistently in separate meetings.

The suggestion that the first task for struggling churches and pastors is to get them to "understand themselves and understand each other" was also inappropriate for St M and Rev E. The boundaries of a fragmenting self tend to shrink to where capacities for calm self-observation, tolerance for complex ideas, and empathy for divergent viewpoints are limited if not absent. Thus a pastoral caregiver working with disintegrating parish selves does not begin by utilizing an introspective, interpretative approach for restoring self cohesion. A caregiver even refrains at this point from offering interpretations regarding the self and its selfobject needs. Kohut helps us see that severely disordered groups and individuals do not become restored ultimately by means of education or instruction per se, but through the availability and empathic responses of highly regarded selfobject figures. Later, when self cohesion is more established, then the disturbing experiences of the parish and pastor can be interpreted. Then comes the time when the security of feeling understood can become strengthened and implemented by understanding via explanations offered by embraced and trusted selfobject caregivers.

In attempting to preserve self cohesion by being a substituting selfobject, a pastoral caregiver functions in ways congruent with present narcissistic needs. Parishes and pastors require massive doses of mirroring, idealizing, or alterego responses. At times a minority within the church may need one type of selfobject response while the majority needs a different type. As much as possible, the pastoral caregiver must be empathically flexible.

A mirror-hungry congregation, for example, may sense renewed well-being when hearing from that caregiver that in the midst of their turmoil they are to be praised: for what they have struggled to do to alleviate their problems, for keeping the barebones of their programs alive, and for being wise enough to ask for help. A pastoral caregiver here offers empathic praise, not hollow words, recognizing that rage, withdrawal, and other disruptive actions are extreme efforts of a crumbling self to hold together.

An idealization-hungry congregation may feel reassured by the presence of a soothing pastoral caregiver: one whose calm demeanor and words mitigate panic; whose perceived strength in body, mind, and spirit is borrowed and merged with for the rekindling of strength in the parish's own self; and whose clear reliance upon God's grace and direction inspires the parish's own devotional life. The supportive caregiver will not repulse efforts to idealize him or her, nor minimize the importance of these responses. Instead, the caregiver to disintegrating parishes will empathically allow and utilize this often temporary idealizing selfobject attachment.

An alterego-hungry parish self may begin to experience renewed self cohesion from a pastoral caregiver who gives warm indications of alterego connections with them: one who joins in with and celebrates openly the parish's unique forms of worship and work; who affirms that the parish and/or pastor still belongs to and is embraced by the wider church who, like them, holds certain beliefs sacred; and who reminds all selves involved that Christ has come to share our common lot and thus we are never alone. These ways of functioning as a mirroring, idealized, or alterego selfobject are not a prelude to the "real work" of restoring self cohesion. They are, instead, central to the "real work" itself, never to be dismissed as merely "setting the stage."

A self psychology understanding of parishes and pastors can inform which religious stories, images, symbols, and metaphors may be most helpful in restoring self cohesion. For instance, the caregiver can be attentive to which revitalizing images of God are most beneficial for self-preservation and restoration. Can a disintegrating parish (or pastor) be sustained best by an image of a providential God who draws persons out of the past and orients them toward the future? In itself it is valuable for persons to be able to honor where they have come from and to project themselves into a healed future understood as the arena of God's grace. But self psychology has helped us see that if, for example, the capacities for a sense of "abiding sameness" dries up (that is, alterego assurances are shattered, as with St M) then efforts to help parishes or pastors restore their selves by "remembering things past" will likely be unproductive. Similarly, while the image of God as the Lord of the Future may evoke hope for change, a disintegrating self's essential hope is for present survival. All energy is given to simply "holding my self together." Perhaps a more fitting image of God needed at the brink of disintegration may be that of the divine selfobject emptying His self and taking up our form, sharing with us our present sufferings and fears, promising to be with us always. In any regard, an organizing image of God is best attuned to the particular narcissistic needs and subjective experiences of the disintegrating parish or pastor.

Pastoral counseling or consulting work with severely fragmenting selves is often difficult. If they call for help at all (which many do not), they look for instant answers. Often they do not follow the advice given them, although they yearn for magic solutions. Some do not give the designated caregiver a chance to stand in their midst as a substituting selfobject. When they do, the caregiver may be barraged with phone calls from various individuals complaining about the pastor or parishioners or denominational leaders.

Part of Kohut's therapeutic goal was to support all types of caregivers by reminding them that work with such fragmented selves is highly complex, physically intense, and often of long duration. Healing results are often of a stationary nature rather than a progressive nature: "Things aren't any worse, but they're not much better, either," said the clerk of the session after the denominational leader had been with them for a while. Progress in such cases tends to be minimal and slow in coming.

Finally, a pastoral caregiver dealing with disintegrating selves must be able to understand the church's and pastor's raw, immature selfobject demands upon her or him, and must be able to respond with optimal empathy to expressions of narcissistic rage and/or narcissistic withdrawal when she or he fails to fulfill selfobject expectations. That's not all. A caregiver must be able to endure not only the church's enervating selfobject demands but also the occasional rise within the caregiver's own self of narcissistic rage and impulses to withdraw. Continual self-care is crucial for every caregiver, never to be ignored.

Immobilized Parish Selves

Other parish selves may be in an immobilized state. Rather than their structure disintegrating, their self lacks motivation. They are stuck. Instead of being in constant crisis over a wide variety of problems, these parish selves have difficulty making decisions on a wide variety of issues—whether to call a new associate, whether to order new hymnals, whether to conduct a financial drive. Their diminished self cohesion is evident in their curtailed capacities for carrying out their core purposes and values, and for enacting their talents beyond minimal levels. Immobilized churches tend to keep the status quo. Some church selves are chronically stymied while other parishes have regressed to this condition of immobilization from previously well-functioning states.

The prognosis for these churches is more positive than cases where the self structure of the parish is seriously defective and prone to further disintegration. Brighter prospects are possible because these churches remain focused around remnants of their firm and functional self. They still have intact goals and purposes, still have some vision of where they want to go, and still speak words of faith—they just cannot put them into action sufficiently or be zestfully energized by them. Furthermore, since the narcissistic energies of the church are not totally absorbed by needs for self-protection or exhausted by bouts of narcissistic rage and/or depressive withdrawal, more energy is available for self-restoration and self-development. As long as a religious community's self benefits from diminished but sufficient mirroring, idealizing, and alterego responses, along with diminished but sufficient capacities for self-regulation when narcissistically injured, that community's self contains healthy potential for remobilization.

The approach of the pastoral caregiver also takes a different focus in this situation. While disintegrating parish selves require a substituting selfobject approach, where the caregiver substitutes for the parish's weak or missing capacities for self-maintenance, the immobilized parish self heals more readily when the caregiver functions as a "problem-solving selfobject," as we term it. Here the caregiver endeavors to restart mobilization by helping the church face and work through persistently unresolved issues that are manifestations of its limbo mode. A disintegrating parish self needs "something done for it" to ward off total collapse, to retain the last strands of self cohesion. The immobilized parish self needs to "begin doing something" that can resurrect the momentum of its intact but inert "nuclear programs and values," as Kohut called those goals that stabilize and energize an individual or group self. A caregiver, therefore, works primarily on concrete problems whose solution will facilitate the remobilization of the parish self.

In this self psychology–informed approach of problem solving, the caregiver is aware of underlying narcissistic difficulties of which specific problems are manifestations. For example, the prime locus of immobilization may be in a chronic longing for selfobject figures no longer available (through death or distance or changed profession), or in repetitive expectations for particular selfobject responses that pastors cannot fulfill, or in long-term difficulties in making use of potentially new selfobjects. Repressed or disavowed narcissistic rage may keep psychological energies secretly horded for retribution. Narcissistic withdraw may curtail energies needed for enactment of nuclear values and ambitions. Hypersensitivity to criticism may stymie efforts to reach out and expose one's efforts. In these cases, the caregiver's primary approach is to deal with the manifestations of these underlying narcissistic fixations.

For example, a parish vacillated over whether or not to even consider whether some female clergy could be their senior minister. The repetitive weighing of pros and cons, the Ping-Pong between one potential decision and another, represented more than an attempt at thorough analysis; it also represented an underlying fear of making a mistake that would be ridiculed by others. Strong mirroring needs and a heightened vulnerability to having one's self-esteem injured were central here. While empathically affirming with the church the normal trepidations involved in such a decision, the caregiver, functioning as problem-solving selfobject, suggested they move from contemplation to action and experience. What they could begin to do was actually make arrangements to experience female pastors first hand. They could go to different churches and worship under the leadership of female pastors. They could ask certain female clergy to substitute for the senior minister when he was gone. They could interview and employ female pastors as interim ministers. The caregiver further helped mobilize action and decision making by suggesting a deadline for deciding one way or another on the issue of a female pastors as senior minister, regardless of uncertainty.

Another parish conducted the same church school program year after year with little zest or success. It operated from a rigid attachment to outdated and limited denominational teaching material, whose removal would be expected to generate intense feelings of guilt and disloyalty to the denomination. Here strong idealizing needs were coupled with a heightened vulnerability for being cut off from one's tower of strength. The consulted caregiver first affirmed how important the denomination was to them and how faithful they had been to it. He then suggested that it would be no breach of loyalty if they conducted a well-crafted survey of their own families, and of families in the surrounding community, in order to at least discover what spiritual needs were most strongly expressed that the church might move to meet. The underlying problem of rigid idealizing attachment was not confronted head on here but was potentially modified by dealing with the specific problem of immobilization in a new, concrete way.

Unlike disintegrating parish selves, an immobilized parish self demonstrates some capacity for self-reflection, and for the ability to endure narcissistic tensions that self-reflection might generate. Consequently, a caregiver might also facilitate mobilization by general empathic explanations of how prior decisions, made as a way of coping with parish tensions (as a way to avoid injures to self-esteem or rejection by admired others, for example), have become the grounds for current immobilization problems. The pastoral caregiver, however, explains in general terms rather than offering deep interpretations of the narcissistic world of the parish or pastor's self.

Once again the caregiver can utilize energizing religious language and symbols in whatever counseling, consulting, or preaching is done in the church. How restorative for immobilized churches, for example, would be the image of a charismatic Jesus casting down demons, throwing out money changers, berating Pharisees, or chastising his own disciples? Just knowing that one belongs to a powerful Christ who overcomes sin and death can alone empower some depleted selves. But individuals and groups who are fragmented do not identify easily with powerful selfobjects who are confidently shaking the world. They do not feel themselves to be that way. Indeed, they often feel the opposite: weak, with no victories in sight.

Instead, immobilized parish selves may be moved more by the image of a puzzled and burdened Jesus, who comes to the Garden of Gethsemane nearly immobilized by the weight of his calling and the painful mission he must face. Here he nearly gives up, nearly stops his aim to live out his purpose in the world. But he does not. Instead he reaffirms his trust in God, gets off his knees, and begins to take one more step forward. Immobilized selves may identify more with this Jesus and be instructed and inspired by his example.

The process of remobilizing church selves usually necessitates less time commitment on the part of the caregiver and less constant selfobject availability than with disintegrating parish selves. Still, there are strong resistances against becoming mobile, even as a parish yearns for it. Old ways are safely known, even if anxiety producing. The caregiver must see these resistances as lingering, archaic efforts to protect self cohesion, and must find creative problem-solving ways to work through and around them.

The pastoral caregiver whose bent is for depth insight counseling may find repetitive work on concrete problems boring, and may thus react with diminished energy and empathy. Stubbornly immobilized churches may also frustrate the caregiver's mirroring need to see grand fruit from hard labor. As always, the caregiver must make efforts to remain firm, functional, and vital within his or her own self.

Devitalized Parish Selves

The selves of other churches may be in a devitalized state. Their prevailing affect (emotional tone) is flat to some degree. While not suffering from self-containment problems (disintegrating parish selves) or from self-enactment problems (immobilized parish selves) they suffer from what we might call "self-joy" problems. For some churches this is a chronic condition. Stated conversely, this is the highest state of self cohesion they have reached. Other churches have regressed to this devitalized state as a result of injuries to their self or erosions of their regulating capacities.

Assessment of this type of disturbed self cohesion is frequently missed or minimized. One enters the church and sees a psychologically firm congregation, whose programs are up and running, whose members exude a certain degree of energy in their worship and service. And yet there is something missing—a lack of innate joy, of relaxed playfulness, of a celebrative spirit. The church self is like an adequate lover whose heart is not "strangely warmed." These churches are sufficiently and productively "acting the Christian's part," but that may also be symptomatic of their self difficulty: there is more acting than abundant living, more going through the motions than being internally animated.

Such churches rarely seek pastoral care help. If they recognize their flat disposition at all, they tend to accommodate to it, to accept it as normal for them. Occasional flurries of overt joy and inspired worship ameliorate, for a time, the sense of psychological devitalization.

Outsiders, however, such as visitors and new pastors, often implicitly pick up on the slightly cold or restrained atmosphere. The church may seem civil but not particularly friendly; accepting but not embracing. Robust hymns and high-volume sermons fail to convince the new listener of spiritual vitality. These varied sensations turned into comments may eventually bring this dispositional state to the church's attention.

For instance, a new pastor with keen perception came to serve a wealthy suburban church renowned for its mission budget. After the excitement of being recruited for the position (his own mirroring needs were being aroused) and temporarily awed by the church's financial power (his idealizing tendencies also became stimulated), he was bewildered by the onset within him of flattened feelings. From careful introspection, he became aware that he was resonating with the emotional ethos of the congregation. In spite of all the energy given for their mission work there was a methodical, business-like plodding along that lacked a sense of innate exuberance. They were productive but not inspired. It was this unrecognized (or denied) disposition that he brought to his church leaders. He asked them to help him help them discover why, given all their blessings, they were bereft of a glow of tangible joy in their life together.

Whereas disintegrating parish selves need something done for them, and immobilized parish selves need to do something, devitalized parish selves need to understand their doing. The primary approach of the caregiver in this situation can be to function as an "illuminating selfobject," as we term it. The denied, unrecognized, or minimized veil of shadows must come to awareness. Holes need to be opened in the church's psychological canopy admitting more inspiring light, more joyful oxygen. These healthily structured and mobilized congregations can find healing grace primarily through illuminating interpretations and explanations regarding their devitalized disposition. Direct use of psychological language and insights, especially informed by self psychology, can be used to help the church understand itself and to open the congregation to more consistent experiences of abundant living.

On the one hand, this illuminating approach is possible because the parish retains strong capacities for self-introspection. On the other hand, this illuminating orientation is appropriate because the problems of devitalized parishes are often centered in how: (1) narcissistic needs of the self give rise to cognitive distortions, and (2) how the self's cognitive distortions give rise to narcissistic reactions. Not only does an individual's or group's narcissistic make-up, experiences with selfobjects, and ability to regulate tensions shape how that self cognitively defines its self-selfobject world, but cognitive misperceptions and misunderstandings go a long way in shaping how the self experiences and evaluates its own and others' selves. Self psychology has helped us understand how fragmentation gives rise to degeneration of language, narrowing of thought, and the abandonment of formerly synthesizing thinking processes.

This is not the place for a thorough discussion of how self disorders and cognitive distortions reinforce each other and, indeed, often give rise to each other. As a brief example, however, narcissistic rage prompts selves to regression to misguided ways of thinking, such as when Rev E was called a "devil." Conversely, distorted ways of thinking also prompt regressions to narcissistic rage. Consistently applying the label "devil" encouraged and elicited reactions of narcissistic rage toward Rev. E. In various ways, relatively mild narcissistic reactions and cognitive distortions are frequently those difficulties keeping a parish in its devitalized state. The illuminating selfobject caregiver tries to bring these to light, and in so doing fosters healing of the narcissistic reactions and the affiliated cognitive defects that impede the parish self from experiencing fuller states of inspired living.

For example, through working with a self psychology informed pastoral caregiver, the minister and leaders of the wealthy suburban church began to realize underlying dynamics in what they were doing. As they began by discussing worship, they were directed to reflect on how they were describing matters (their cognitive patterns). Many comments contained references to "us" and "them." "We don't have 'emotional' services like those other churches do. Our members are more comfortable with a dignified approach." "We tend to focus on understanding the gospel while they seemed more interested in physical experiences." What they slowly realized was that they operated out of a cognitive style that unhealthily divided the world into "us" and "them." In addition to that, they also began to grasp their tendency to operate out of an either/or way of thinking: worship is either this way or that way; you can worship either as we do or you can worship as they do. As a result, they had cognitively cut themselves off from other ways of entering into worship and other ways of making their whole self newly vitalized.

In addition to this dawning realization came a harder admission, a narcissistic one. For as much as they prided themselves on being open-minded, they really did think their way of worship was most proper—not just for themselves but in general. They operated out of a mild state of what Kohut calls "grandiosity," a condition of feeling superior to others. Their worship style became part of their pride, and thus their self-identity, and any serious shaking of that espoused identity was a threat to their self cohesion. This mild narcissistic disorder, therefore, also impeded openness to new possibilities for being infused with experiences of self-joy—self-joy that they not only lacked but were also apprehensive of getting. Too much exuberance, too much spirit, was not only "not us" but also a threat to their secure sense of self.

This parish's work with the illuminating selfobject caregiver helped remove barriers to fuller self experiences. As their eyes cleared, the caregiver stepped back into a supportive role, letting the pastor and leaders absorb the insights and discuss what this might mean for them. There was still a ways to go, but they were now on the right road, and they were going in the right direction. There was joy just in that.

One more brief example: An inner-city church functioned well but seemed vaguely glum. The pastoral caregiver listened both for the cognitive ways in which the church body spoke about itself and for hints of its underlying narcissistic struggles. What emerged was the prevalence of a devitalizing cognitive distortion. While enjoying relative success as a church, many members harkened back to a previous "golden age" when parish life was "exceedingly good." "That time is over and gone," was the general cognitive conclusion. "We will never be like that again." "How we are now is how we will continue to be. We might as well get use to it." The cognitive distortion here was "permanentizing"—this is the way things are and they will permanently be this way forever; nothing will change; there is no hope for something better or like what we had. What this implicitly operating cognitive distortion did was to undercut openness to being joyfully infused again. There was no sense making their self available to new sources of inspiration because they would be fleeting at best.

But what was the underlying narcissistic issue that prompted (or sustained) this pervasive cognitive distortion? Once again through empathic listening the caregiver realized that a majority of the congregation was in a mild state of grief. A greatly beloved pastor, with them for forty-five years, become ill and died. He had been their idealized selfobject whose smile and manner, wise words and flowing sermons, had founded a "golden age" within their hearts. And so with his death their hearts had stopped, as it were. And as grieving persons often do, they lamented in language that subtly declared the permanence of their current grief experience—"This diminished way of life will last forever." It's difficult to be up when your ways of thinking and your narcissistic struggles are working against you. It was this that the caregiver gently illuminated.

A great deal of narcissistic gratification can accrue to the pastoral caregiver from working with the devitalized type of parish self. Here grand fruit often does come from hard labor. Ready compliments and expressions of thanks (mirroring responses) also abound as parish life improves These are to be enjoyed. A caregiver's self, however, may expand into a grand sense of wisdom—if not superiority—in this situation. Slaps on the back can go to the head. As a result, a caregiver may be reluctant to leave such warmly mirroring environments which, when leaving happens, may lead to some devitalization of the caregiver's own self.

Realistic appraisal suggests that elements of dysfunction, disequilibrium, and forces moving toward depletion may be as pervasive in the church as its healthy attributes. The former conditions need not be a despairing realization for us, just a painfully focusing one.

At the same time, no matter how fragmented, churches possess remnants of a self-righting capacity. To some degree they are aware of having shifted away from their central ministry and are drawn to reorient themselves to their calling. Stated in self psychology terms, they sense having lost their cohesion and strive to regain their equilibrium. In so doing they move toward a state of holy wholeness, fulfilling the promise given us that we might have life, and have it abundantly.

6

First Interview with Heinz Kohut

Chicago, March 22, 1981

Randall: Would you start by relating when and how your interest in religion or religious issues originated?

Kohut: I don't think that I could honestly say that religion is one of my foremost preoccupations. It's really not. But since I'm interested in human beings and *their* preoccupations, in what makes them tick, what's important to them, and what's on their minds, obviously religion is a powerful force in life. It has been an essential aspect of human existence as long as there has been any knowledge of human activity at all. So, naturally I'm interested in it as a student of people.

Now, my impression is that you are not interested so much, and rightly so I think, in, let us say, the clinical aspects of religious beliefs. In other words, it is clear that every psychiatrist, every psychoanalyst, and every therapeutic helper to people will, in the course of his years of experience, encounter people to whom religion will mean a great deal or has meant a great deal or whose parents' religiosity made a particular imprint on them, for better or worse. So those would be clinical issues. But I don't think that is your focus and it is not my focus. It would be a highly specialized research project. You are interested in how I view religion as a psychological force in human beings.

Let's start this way. We are not examining this topic as it were from scratch; we are not examining this topic as if nothing had ever been said about it. We are examining it specifically, I would think, against a background of the traditional views of modern depth psychology, specifically, of course, of Freud's, and his opinions, and the majority of analysts' opinion, of depth psychologist's opinions, of religion. You cannot, as a psychoanalyst, which I am, as a depth psychologist that I am, talk about religion and disregard that *The Future of an Illusion* has been written, disregarding the wholesale condemnation of religion by Freud. Within this framework I would agree there is a justified condemnation of religion—within this framework, I say.

Now what is that framework? I'm letting myself go. You can't expect me to give you a lecture that is prepared or a manuscript of something I've thought about. I've not actually thought about it at all. I let myself go free. On the other hand, this is a topic to which I have given some thought over the years.

What Freud did, and what he did in error, was that he applied the yardstick of scientific values to religion. If you judge religion as a science it is a ridiculous science. It has not always been a ridiculous science but it is now a ridiculous science. Originally I would think—again I'm not a cultural anthropologist, although I have my own ideas about the development of culture—originally the borderlines between what we now call science and what we now call art and what we now call religion were not very sharp. I think originally it was one conglomerate, or better still, not a conglomerate, for conglomerate implies the amalgamation or the putting together and mixing together of already developed units. But it was as it were a "potentiality" that, seen in retrospect, pointed in three different directions. I think these must now be, in order to give proper meaning to science, art, and religion, these must now be more or less, not totally but more of less, be separated.

In other words, let us say religion as a science is to be condemned in some way. If religion explains the origin of the universe to my mind in a particular circumscribed way, as the act of a human-like or humanoid god that decides to create the world in seven days, strictly dividing one day after another, that's phony science. And it doesn't do any good to say it's metaphor or twist it or turn it. That makes it artistically worked over; but let's call a spade a spade. Where religion tries to be science, the scientist from his point of view has a right to say, "Don't try to compete with your insufficient means with us. That's ridiculous. These are ridiculous results. This is fairytale."

But this is not religion. It doesn't mean that one cannot allow it as a part and parcel of a whole that has its history, et cetera. But when I talk about the value of religion, I'm not talking about the fairytale science of religion. And when Freud objected to religion as the future of an illusion, the mistake he made was that he evaluated it as if it were a science.

As a science it is an abominably poor science. Its explanations do not hold water to scientific explanations. Every bit of honestly admitted not-knowing by scientists is a million times better than the knowing of the religious believer in terms of explanations of one's surroundings. So, in that sense Freud was right. However, where he was completely in error is that he judged religion as if it were a science. That is not what religion is all about. This is not why man needs and creates religions. It is only a perversion of religion, of true religion, to make it into a competitor of science. The Monkey Trial, that's ludicrous religion. The one has nothing to do with the other.

Now, I'm not a purist. If in the course of a lifetime of growth in each individual one begins with allegories of the creation of the world, or something of that order, then, indeed, it becomes built into a kind of metaphorical meaning that is quite compatible, side by side, with what Freud considered the only attitude worth having, namely the scientific worldview. But Freud never explained, at least to my knowledge—and I could see how he would explain it if he had—how great scientists can at the same time be religious people. He would have said they split them-selves into some nonsense versus some logical functioning, and this is the only way in which it can be explained.

My point of view is that the split isn't such a split. Why should not one have a religious feeling about existence and yet at the same time pursue scientific investigation? One is really unrelated to the other, just as art is unrelated. Science deals with cognitive issues, with explanations. Art deals with beauty, creating beautiful things, pleasing things. And re-ligion is neither the one nor the other.

Now what is religion? Let me tell you about another concept that I have. One of the key concepts, if not *the* key concept, much misunder-stood and, on the basis of misunderstanding, maligned, is the concept of the *selfobject*. First, selfobject is not a person. Selfobject, if anything, is a function of a person. It is the way a person is specifically perceived. The same person can be a love object and a selfobject, at the same time or at different times. When one is married one's wife is a love object. You love her, you want to give her things, you want to get things from her, whether its children or gifts. You admire her looks, whatever . . . her way of behaving, her poise. Those are the things you love. But many times she's a selfobject. When you're in trouble she will understand and grasp that you come home and are burdened, and will not respond, "Snap out of it! I've been busy all day. Don't burden me with your burdens." But she will see that at the moment you need more than I and will give it. And the other way around: you will serve as her selfobject when she's in need of shoring up. This is not love. It can be quite compatible with love, but it isn't really love. When I help my patients—and I think I help them considerably—I can't say I love them. I don't want anything from them and I don't want them to love me. If they love me I examine that, not to debunk it, but this is grist for the mill of my understanding of them, and their conflicts about their loving me. But I don't *want* to be loved. This is not the type of relationship it is. The same way as parents toward children are mainly functioning as their selfobjects. They're enjoying vicariously their growth. Now loosely speaking all this is often called love, but that isn't love. That (being a selfobject) is a very specific function. It is the hatching, nourishing, nurturing of a growing self, up to a point.

Why do I speak about selfobjects? Because selfobjects are a need that people have from the first to the last breathe. It isn't anything one can ever grow out of. The myth of independence and autonomy is something I often try to fight. There is no such thing as life without this (selfobject) kind of responsiveness; there is no psychological survival unless one has this kind of responsiveness. If one has too little of it for any long period of time, one becomes depressed. One begins to feel empty. One can't survive—(those) people who have been treated without any empathical resonance at all.

And *empathy*, of course, is a key concept again. It doesn't mean necessarily to be nice on the basis of empathy. It certainly doesn't need to be confused with compassion. To be understood is quite compatible with hostile purposes. I can understand you in order to cheat you the better. But the strange thing is that even to be understood for hostile purposes is better than not to be understood at all. The devastating effects of a very few human experiences, such as we now have unfortunately in this century seen in the prolonged detention in concentration camps, for example, was not the hostility of the guards to the victims, but the *utter* disregard for them. It wasn't being killed; it was being exterminated, which is very different from being killed. What are exterminated? Insects. Cockroaches. We do this without much empathy for our cockroaches, yet human beings even have *that* a little bit. It moves like us, it's frightened like us when it's attacked, it rushes and has something like anxiety in it. In a way we are not totally empathy-less even with the insects we kill. But when we walk and step on an insect we don't give it much thought. It was this experience that made the survivors of these experiences—the handful of survivors—so *utterly* degraded, so utterly beyond the scope of real psychological help in most instances. That is why I so often quote Kafka's insight into the destroyed self, the famous metamorphosis story of Gregory Samsa, who wakes up in the morning and he is a cockroach. The important thing is that his parents in the next room speak of him in the third-person singular—"He did this and he did that"—angrily, and you can see why he's a cockroach, because he didn't evoke the welcoming joy and the pride in his parents, but their utter disregard for him. That is why his self has changed. When Mr. K, I believe it is, in *The Trial*, is finally executed, first of all he never found out what he is guilty about, and secondly, when he is being executed the executioners say "Like a dog" as they turn the knife in his chest. The point is that he is not treated as human. To be made guilty is *paradise* by comparison to this utter disregard. In *The Castle*, too, he is searching and searching to get to "them" in the castle, but they are non-approachable. It reminds me of some of the poor rich people's children who I now treat, who grew up on the wealthy North Shore, whose parents were always unapproachable. They were playing bridge, going out. There was nobody but hired help but you could never get at them (the parents).

It is this that we mean when we say one needs selfobjects all one's life. Once you grasp this, you grasp a great deal. If you tell somebody who is dying, "You're an example to me, the way you face death. You know, we all cross that threshold one day and, boy, I hope I can face it as you do," then you have helped that person. It is the only real help, or something on that order, that you give, particularly if you really mean it. In other words, you have put together his self, his pride, his sense, "Aha, I'm quite a guy dying here." Out of something that is utterly depressing otherwise, if people (also) withdraw from you because they don't want to be reminded that they will have to die someday, too, it has to be the remaining in contact that helps.

If you read in my discussion with Professor Heller in our exchange of letters [*Psychoanalysis and the Interpretation of Literature*], I quote there that particular event among the astronauts when their spaceship was damaged and there was very much doubt whether it could maneuver at all or whether the re-entry into the earth could be managed without the ship burning up because they might not be able to fire slowdown rockets. They decided that even though they could live much longer by circling in empty space, that they would much rather burn up in the earth's atmosphere, knowing at least in their dying moments that they were back again to where they belonged, in a human atmosphere. Death or no is not the important issue. So, it's a roundabout way of coming to my actual point that is more related to the issue of religion.

Among the selfobjects that human beings have and need, which is an extremely important and not yet a sufficiently investigated point, are what I call the *cultural selfobjects* of the person. We are continuously surrounded not only by personal selfobjects—wife and friends and what have you—but also by what I call the cultural selfobjects: admired composers if you're musical, present and past; admired writers present and past; great scientists whom you emulate, present and past. You name it. Political heroes, courageous men that infused courage into you by looking at their example. Just think of the *enormous*, the pivotal, the crucial importance that Churchill had in this century. Where would we be if this man had not at that particular moment, when the end of all culture as we knew it and had sustained us, seemed to be in sight, and a new, brutal, as it seemed to most of us, nonhuman culture was taking over, that we had nothing to do with, that we could never fit into anymore. At that moment there was a man who was visibly unafraid, who visibly one hundred percent subscribed to the culture of Western civilization, and around whom clustered all the courage that was left in the rest of us. When Hitler said he would turn the British chicken's neck, Churchill said, "Some chicken. Some neck." You could see his own neck. That was something to identify with. There was vigor of his selfobject. I don't know if he was a great planner or statesman, but he was a paradigm of power, strength, and fearlessness at that moment, a willingness to fight. And for that people gladly die and they die really gladly. We can gladly die and unhappily live, there is no question about that. It has been talked about and written about from *The Red Badge of Courage* on, in a variety of ways. Sartre was interested in that, too.

But anyway, among the great selfobjects, the great cultural selfobjects of man—and this, of course, is what I'm aiming at—is religion. And I think that religion cannot be evaluated as science primarily. It cannot even, as I think some religious people do, be evaluated as a first cousin to art. I don't mean to say that I disregard all ritual. Certain ritual in religion seems to be an almost intrinsic part of religion, although that would be an artistic aspect of religion. It certainly has more of that to it than science has, although I would say that good science should also have a bit of artistic quality. It has often been said that great hypotheses are convincing not only by their explanatory value but simultaneously by their gracefulness, by the sparingness of the means that they employ, by the harmony of what is being presented. Why shouldn't great scientific writing be written in good language, in beautiful language, in rhythmical language? And some is and some isn't. Obviously it is only secondary, and the same is true for religion.

I don't think the beauty aspects of religion are the essence of religion, and where it becomes the essence of religion, then people with true religious spirit will try to cleanse it from the excess of ritual. Apart from all the political and other issues involved in the Reformation, I believe that was part of it, that Luther felt that a shift had taken place from the essentials of religion to peripheral issues, that there was more ritual, more pomp and circumstance, issues of that particular type. And as you know full well, although there are all shades of Catholicism, Catholicism on the whole has a perhaps greater admixture of the artistic in religion than, let us say, the Protestant religion. But there is an overlap, obviously. There are very non-artistic facets or layers in Catholicism and there is a bit of pomp and circumstance in, let us say, the Episcopalian church. I don't know if I'm saying this exactly right but you can fill in, flesh out what I'm saying from your much vaster knowledge of religion itself.

To my mind, to make a very long story short, the only way in which psychology in general, and self psychology, of course, par excellence, can and must evaluate religion and can explain the significance of religion is by seeing it as one of the three great cultural selfobjects of man: science, art, and religion, each of them fulfilling *totally* different needs of man.

Now, in what way does religion fulfill this need? Well, in innumerable ways, and a lot depends, of course, to what particular cultural layer, to what particular needs, the various religions address themselves in man. As selfobjects, a cultural selfobjects, the religious institutions fulfill a function to shore up, to hold together, to sustain, to make harmonious, to strengthen, man's self. Some people need more of that and some need less of that. I believe, however, that seen in the *broadest* possible way, no one can do and does do without religion in one form or another. I don't mean it in terms of organized religion. I don't mean it in terms of social institutions. But I would say, for example, that psychoanalysis has more than its share of being a religion, and I think that what is wrong with psychoanalysis in that respect is really the counterpoint of Freud's attack on religion. By trying to dispense totally with even accepting religion as a powerful and meaningful and value force in human life, it came in as it were through the back door; so that instead of its being only a search for psychological truth, it became burdened with a sense of, what should I say, excessive loyalty to the originator, to the founder of psychoanalysis, to certain maxims that he held, instead of the mere gratitude and admiration for a great scientist and now let's go on from there. It is very much more difficult in psychoanalysis as compared, for example, to physics. No physicist in his right mind would think that Newton, who was probably the greatest scientist who ever lived, is in any way demeaned by the total shift of interest in modern physics from the macrocosm and the interaction of huge stellar bodies and gravitation, to the microcosm of matter and how matter is composed, that follows totally different laws, is totally at odds with the laws that Newton had discovered. Does it mean, therefore, that we have rebelled against Newton? We couldn't be where we are without the dwarf on the shoulders of the giant. It's really not a very good allegory, because there are giants on the shoulders of giants in science. I cannot say that Planck is smaller than Newton, or Einstein is smaller than Newton, or that Heisenberg is smaller than Newton. These are people with enormous capacities who moved us forward in our understanding and our capacity to explain the external world in a particular way. And our admiration for Newton is totally undiminished. The grasp of the solar system by Copernicus is as admirable today, knowing full well that it was in error, as it should have been in Copernicus's day. At least this limited part of the universe it could recognize. That the whole solar system moves, that there are millions of solar systems—that is a different story. He explained one thing at a time, but that was an enormous advance.

And the same is true for Freud. I don't want to go into analysis now. Analysis is an important science and an enormously successful science. It moves forward, but it is a bit burdened, and more burdened I believe than most other branches of science by an excessive loyalty to previous ideas. By that I don't mean to argue against conservatism, because a degree of conservatism is necessary. Not every Tom, Dick, and Harry can come every day and throw overboard everything and say, "Now we are starting over from scratch again." That has to be done from time to time when real need arises and new phenomenon claim attention that are not properly explained by previously explanatory models. Then you include those and explain those, then maybe you see the former explanatory models in a somewhat different light.

The same is true, I believe, with self psychology in the examination of the narcissistic disorders, the self disturbances. At first it dealt with a comparatively delimited number of phenomena that we observe, but then, in retrospect, we could apply it even to previous insights and see them from a different vantage point so that the overall theory changed, not only the theory as it applied to a small group of phenomena.

So, my impression again is—and I'm circling around the center—that when we examine religion and ask ourselves about the significance of religion, and I mean *significance*, not *importance*. . . . Importance we know. There are many things that are important to people, from sports to candy bars, but they are not significant. Sports may be significant. Candy bars are hardly significant, although they may be significant, too, in terms of the significance that it has in making up for insufficient maternal care and then having something that culture supplies from machines. Instead of the mother, at least one can thrown something into a machine that is then maternal to you and spews out something that tastes sweet and is good. So, the significance in investigating, for example, the meaning of the candy bar dispensing machine. You could write a paper on it. I don't know if people have done it or not but it could easily be done, obviously.

Now, religion is obviously a much broader supportive system, as is art or as is science to man in this respect. But it is an enormously important supportive system. If this were known and understood. . . . And I'm really seeing you and talking to you because I have the feeling that you have an inquisitive mind and an open mind, and that you have crossed your own field and are able to reach out to something thought up by somebody like myself who comes from a different field, although since you do psychotherapy you are a cousin as it were. But still, you come to it from a different direction. I come to it from medicine, from having worked in inorganic neurology. . . . I mean in organic neurology, but not from a psychological field, from a non-psychological field. You come from religion to the healing. That is why this fancy word of yours [*soteriological*] that I had to look up in the dictionary and that everyone looks up in the dictionary who sees your paper—it's a good eye-catching devise—is a beautiful bridging concept, like *selfobject*. With a little twist you can look at it more from the religious point of view; with another little twist you can look at it from a psychotherapeutic [point of view]. What is healing? What cluster of meanings does the word *healing* have? You can talk of it in terms of *the* Savior and salvation; you can talk about it in terms of taking out gallstones by the aid of a particular technique that a surgeon uses. But obviously you would not dignify a surgeon with this particular word, but you could dignify his attitude toward life in surgery in that particular way. If he were a passionate healer, if he went out like Schweitzer into the sticks of Africa, then we come to a closer wedding of the two meanings again that the word *soteriological* has. Is that how it is pronounced?

What I'm saying in the usual vernacular is that it is a two-way street and not a one-way street. Not only should self psychologists and psychologists in general appreciate the meaning that religion has in the maintenance of man's self, but, on the other hand, people engaged in religious activities as ministers, as healers within a religious framework, that they too should broaden and deepen their self-understanding about the meaning of their functions.

While any new knowledge tends at first to be disturbing—you know, the old story about the centipede who becomes aware of his feet and can't walk. . . . Are you a tennis player? Okay. If you are a tennis player and have a certain style and somebody teaches you a new style that is in fact better, for a while you will play abominably. Or piano, if you learn a new technique. You have done pretty well with your poor technique, and in the interim you will be poor, and in the end it will be on a higher level.

The same is true here, too. People have a natural resistance against burdening themselves with new insight, particularly when they are already, as it were, in a particular swing, that it will interfere with their gait—and it will, but temporarily, and then it will lift them up to a higher level. So, if the insights concerning the self sustaining aspects of religion, that people in the religious field—professionals in the religious field if I may use that term—have intuitively employed, I think that in the long run—in the medium run I would even say, it wouldn't have to be quite so long as all that; it wouldn't take generations, it would take a bit of work and working through—I think they would come out ahead if they would study our contributions in depth, as you are trying to make them do. That is the value, it seems to me, of your contributions.

And I like the dialogue. I like the dialogue not because I think that so much comes from debate and discussion. I'm leery about that. I don't have the impression that much really what is creative ever comes out of arguments. But one has to be, what should I say, *semi-permeable*. You have to allow enough input to stir you up but not so much that you are continuously on the defensive and argue and have to prove your point. Then you never have time to develop something within yourself. It is this kind of give and take between, let us say, especially my branch of depth psychology and religion, that they could fruitfully engage in, in interchange of ideas and meanings and feelings, and investigate what we are doing that your cover word *soteriological* addresses itself to really very nicely. I smiled when I saw the word because it seemed so highfalutin, but once I caught on, you know, I had the feeling that, well, really it was a good word to choose, like *selfobject* is a good word to choose, which is also often demeaned. But once you understand what it is, it becomes indispensable, in abbreviated use and in easing communication.

Now the real question is how to examine in detail what the contribution is that religion specifically makes to the holding together, the strengthening, the harmonizing of man's self in general and, of course, in particular in our time and in our regions. When we say "in our time" we must also say "in our culture." It is clear that religion in Tibet, and religion in, let us say, Poland, at this moment, is a totally different influence than religion has at the University of Chicago, to use an extreme example, in which anybody's open claim that he is a very religious person would make him suspect among his colleagues. But if he explains what he is after, that's a different story. Rockefeller Chapel at Easter time is reasonably filled and it's reasonably filled by faculty. Of course it's only at Easter. On a regular Sunday, you know, I've rarely seen it filled. I don't go very often myself, but I occasionally have gone when there is some stirring preacher. I listened to Karl Barth once and it was a moving sermon. That's years and years ago. And Pastor Niemoeller was here once and I heard him and it was a very moving occasion. That's just two people who happened to be here. One time Martin Buber gave a lecture that wasn't a religious service. At least I saw Martin Buber, although I didn't understand a single word of what he was talking about for an hour and a half, and I don't mean acoustically. Still, I had the feeling it was an event; it was very strange.

At any rate, what is it, specifically, that religion gives to man that results in these results? I will not and cannot—and you wouldn't expect me on short notice and ad hoc basis—to give you some well-thought-out results and answers to this question. I would say, "That's your baby—yours and other peoples.'" I've given a framework. Whether that framework fits this particular task or not totally I do not know. But the framework is still there. When I say, for example, "hold together, harmonize, strengthen," speaking about the self, then I'm falling back on a framework that is already established: the three particular areas of dysfunction of the self; that it is fragmenting, that it is weak, that it is chaotic and disharmonious. But there are many, many other qualities that one could fasten on. No question that for many people when they go and hear an uplifting sermon they are lifted beyond the humdrum of everyday existence. They feel that they are living on a higher level, at least for a while, identifying, as it were, with the meaning that has been given to them. The mere unrolling of specific holidays in the course of a twelve-month period, like the unrolling of the seasons, the rebirth at Easter spring, the gradual decline with winter, and the again rebirth with Easter spring, appeals to something deep in all of us. And all religion has something of that. So uplifting, for example, is an important thing.

What is uplifting? Uplifting, as you probably realize from having read my work, begins with the mother uplifting the baby and holding it close to her. The baby is frightened, disheveled, fragmented. The mother is calm, big, powerful. The baby is lifted up, held close; it merges with the mother's calmness. If religion can *uplift* a person by letting him merge with some sense of broad meanings, with values that are lasting, that are beyond the humdrum of earning another buck and being depressed because the stocks in which one has invested in have gone down, or a paper of yours was rejected for publication, or whatever narcissistic injuries we all suffer from, we become more harmonized again. Some people just need to go into a church and sit there. Some people get a religious feeling on a mountain top or looking down the Grand Canyon, or walking through the woods. Some people get a religious feeling by listening to great music that is not predominately the beauty of the music but gain this kind of broad uplifting quality.

That's why I said at first there is some degree of overlap between art and religion, even between art and science.

So we divide up, as you know, the functions of selfobjects into three groups. [First is] the merger with the idealized selfobject. [Second is] the responsiveness to our own vitality and ambitions and our sense of innate greatness, which religion sometimes refers to as *grace*, I believe. In other words, that there is something given to you, some innate perception of your right to be here and to assert yourself, and that somebody will smile at you and will respond to you and will be in tune with your worthwhileness—that is parental and that is *soteriological* probably in your sense. And there is, finally, what I call the twinship support or the alterego support—just to be surrounded by people who feel and think likewise, to sing in the choir, to be a member of a congregation.

I'm talking about every gross experience that may sound ridiculous to a professor of theology who examines this or that detail of religious dogma. But when it comes that way, remember that the science of religion is not religion. A historian of religion is a scientist. The standards I would judge him by are the standards of a scientist. Does he report accurately? Does he show sequences of thought and development in an explanatory way, in a meaningful and correct way? These are his standards. It's very different from the religious feeling that sustains somebody who gives his sermon, particularly in difficult times.

Or, we were talking about HM. I know he is probably a troubled man from what I've heard, that he went through a great deal of personal upheaval himself. Whether its true or not I don't know; I've just heard that. But I don't care what he went through. The more the merrier. It is only when one has firsthand experience with suffering that one can truly be in touch with other people's needs. There are people who are so well put together and so walled off, fine and admirable, but they don't give you anything. The greatness of Dostoevsky in his novels shows that he can have deep understanding for the most troubled individuals. If you want to read anything at all, among all my writings, although I don't think it mentions religion more than in passing, there are two that will give you the best access to my attitude toward all this. The one is my lecture called *The Psychoanalyst in the Community of Scholars* and the other one is my exchange of letters with Professor Heller. You would have to do your own translating job and how it applies in a different sense, although I believe

I did refer directly to religion in my debate with Heller, who attacked analysis unmercifully, and I came to the defense of analysis as science.

Let us leave it at this today. After listening to the tape and having the transcript typed up, it would seem better to meet at another time to go over questions you might have.

7

Second Interview with Heinz Kohut

Chicago, April 12, 1981 (Palm Sunday)

Randall: Our last meeting focused on religion more as a cultural selfobject that supported and encouraged man's sense of self. I'd like to focus today on religion as an *expression* of man's creative self, how it arises from man's own personality, from within his self. You alluded a couple of times in the Heller letters to religion as both an expression of man as well as a support to his sense of self. We focused very well, you did, on religion as a cultural selfobject. What about religion as an expression of the self?

Secondly, from studying your writings I find that most of the time religion is discussed in terms of the self's relation to idealized selfobjects. Is that the dominate sector of the self in which you find religion operative?

Kohut: I don't know what particular pronouncements of mine, either in our last interview or in my writings, you have in mind. But once you posed that (last) question, I would have no doubt that anything as encompassing and broad and basic as religion is to man—for that matter as art is to man, or for that matter as science is to man—could not possibly relate to just one dimension of the self. While I would say that perhaps the most conspicuous and most easily noticeable dimension of religion, namely man's relationship to God, is that of an idealization of being uplifted by an idealized other. This is by no means the only aspect of the support that man gets from religion, or if you wish, from the construction, the creation, of religion by man.

You see, we are dealing now with two very different questions, and yet they are terribly interrelated of course. You challenge me, in terms of a good challenge, not an attacking challenge, you challenge me appropriately, in responding to the questions: (a) Is only idealization involved, and (b) Aren't there two directions in the importance of, the position of, religion as one examines it? One can, of course, examine it as a creation of man's mind and man's needs, and one can also then examine the influence that the creation of man's mind and needs has on man secondarily. We are talking, up to now, mainly of religion as it exists and what it means of man born *into* a humanity in which religion is already established. I have no doubts about the fact that religion was created by man's mind in a certain sense. I have no doubt that religion continues to be created by man's mind, changed, altered according to needs, that encompasses responses not only to the idealized selfobject and man's needs for idealized selfobjects, but also responses to, let us say, the other aspects of the self: the alter-ego aspects of the self, to be surrounded by likeminded ones or similar ones; and the sense of being responded to and not being alone, that there is an *acceptance* in the world of one's arriving, of one's life, or one's personality [*mirroring selfobject responses*].

In other words, my response to both of your challenges is, yes, you are quite right. That has to be examined, too. It is not the most conspicuous and the most immediately inviting issue, but it is probably equally important to the one we have up to now discussed the most.

The question is where to start. Let me, helter-skelter at first, continue on the receiving side, on man's receiving side—what does religion do for him—before we go into how does he creates it, how religion is an expression of his self.

The idealizing aspects, those are clear. Everything that I had written about messianic leaders, everything that I had written about charismatic leaders, can be translated into some form or other into the institution, into the existing cultural organization of religion. A religion, to my mind—well, even there one would have to be a little bit careful—but it is clear that what we generally mean by religion can hardly dispense with the concept of God, because there must be something idealizeable, something that nears perfection or that is perfect, something that one wants to live up to, something that lifts one up. So it would not be easy, at any rate, for me to envision a religion that dispenses with the God concept. It is not unthinkable, but it's certainly not what one finds among the many, many religions of man. Certainly when we talk about the God concept it is, on the one hand, something to be looked up to and something uplifting to you, something into which you can merge, to which you can retreat. And it is a stabilizing force in an otherwise unpredictable world, and one that has some very tangible psychological effects on many people.

Let me mention one example out of many. Perhaps the most devastating experience that an adult man—by adult man I don't mean gender—an adult man or woman can be exposed to happened in this century under the totalitarian Hitler regime, namely the concentration camp experience, in particular the exposure to what significantly was called *extermination policies.* Now I happen to read at the present time a story or a book by a Polish writer, who won the Nobel Prize not so long ago for literature, by the name of Milosz, who describes the goings-on in Poland during the time of the Nazi occupation and the extermination camps and the mentality toward those to be exterminated. Now death is not in and of itself scary, I believe. I do not believe that a healthy individual is afraid of death, that a well-balanced individual is afraid of death. I believe that the ultimate of mental health relates to an inner perception of the normal life curve, of being born, of growing, of reaching some flowering of the program that's laid down in us early in life, and a fading away and ultimately extinction. I do not believe that a person that one can call a psychologically healthy person is unduly afraid of dying. But there are conditions that have to be spelled out.

First of all, I believe that any looking at a human being in isolation is an artifact—there is no such thing. There is no baby in isolation, there is no middle-aged person in isolation, and there is no dying person in isolation. It is always the person surrounded by the matrix of selfobjects that we are talking about. I always use the example of physiological being. You cannot subtract physiological being from the normal matrix of oxygen that we breathe. Obviously we are born to be surrounded by oxygen. You cannot examine a body, the physiology of a body, in isolation of oxygen. He is born *for* oxygen, and for many other things that surround him—for certain temperature range and what have you—and only in this kind of milieu is he, he.

The same is true psychologically. A baby is never a baby alone. A baby is never weak, therefore. A normal baby is strong because the normal baby includes the caretakings and responses of selfobjects that are empathically fitted with him.

Now this is true at any stage of life and this is certainly true as one nears death. The fear of death in many instances, at least that I know about, is the fear of the loss of the support of selfobjects. People tend to withdraw from the dying person. If you do not withdraw, if you give the person appropriate selfobject responses, not as a learned technique but as a genuine response of one human being to another—let us say, for example, but really only as an example, "You're dying. I will also cross that threshold one of these days. The way you handle this is an inspiration to me. I will get a great deal of strength from watching how you do this"—that person who hears that will feel confirmed in his dying self. He will feel pride in having given something to the next generation, in teaching them how to face death courageously, and satisfied with having lived out the program of his life. I mean, this is only an example of selfobject support and you can easily translate this into the terms of religion.

What support does religion give to the dying person? Now take, for instance, such a gimmick—let us say, in the broadest sense—as the "after life"—that there will be a heaven into which the virtuous will go. Let's forget about the guilty man and the punishment and what have you—hell, et cetera—but just simply an afterlife, a denial of the fact that one really dies. Is this true or is this not true? From the scientific point of view, within the compass of this kind of scientific reality, it's an error, it's a falsification of reality and as such it is appropriately to my mind rejected by science. Man does not have an afterlife anymore than the rose has. There is a seed, there is a flowering, there is a wilting, there is a death and the next generation of roses takes over. I think that one isn't really fully alive if one doesn't somehow down deep in one's bones feel this eternal rhythm of life, this coming and going of which one is only a link in a chain. To me this is an uplifting thought, not a discouraging thought. It goes beyond my individuality to something broader and more enduring than this little me that is common, hasn't been here during Plato's time and will not be here in a thousand years when there's another Plato or maybe nothing. Who knows? Why do I have to be around and have been around? I wasn't and I won't. That doesn't disturb me.

But what is the truth about it? The truth to my mind is that there are enduring issues in this world, that there is the enduring power of creation and re-creation of life, that somehow puzzlingly life arose and the complexity and beauty of human experience arose, that this is not accidental, but that this will in somehow and in someway endure, whether I happen to observe it or not. This to my mind is symbolized in a way in a sense of talking about eternal life. The fairy tale of a heaven with lots of winged creatures singing hallelujah, that doesn't particularly send me. I think that's a rather boring existence. This is very different from what really gives life its zest and its beauty and I can't imagine that this would be so beautiful. You know, like, take music. A chord is nice. But how long can you listen to a chord? It's the living, the ups and the downs and the final fading, *that* is the beauty of great music, not a forever-continued perfect chord. It seems to me a life that would never end, always in bliss singing the praise of the Lord in heaven, to me would be a come down; it is not an uplifting image to me.

Religion is present on many levels and on many layers and it speaks in different languages to different ears, and what may be couched in very simple language—in fairy tale language, and as far as science is concerned, in falsifying language—may still contain a kernel of very important truth in a different sense: that there are values, there is something enduring about it, there is something timeless about certain things. And I think that is really much, much more important and much, much harder to express. The greatness of an experience is in fact timeless. It can happen at any time. It has nothing to do with time. The value of something is always valuable whether the people think it or not, whether the human race is or will be extinct one day or not. I suppose that the Darwinian evolution is essentially a true concept, may be changed and may be of different ideas at some other time, but the probability it seems to me is likely.

So, in other words, the idealized dimensions of the God concept are on the highest philosophical level, it seems to me, an expression—and here we come to the creative side of human experience and of human self—an expression of the recognition that there is something about this world in our experience that does lift us up beyond the simplicity of an individual existence, that lifts us into something higher, enduring, or as I would rather say, timeless.

Now, are there other dimensions, then, of religion beyond the idealized God concept? I would think so. We talk about three types of selfobjects—not that there are not many others, but my classification narrows things down and one can branch out from there. There are the idealized selfobjects, the mirroring selfobjects, and the alterego or twin-ship selfobjects. Let's go from the idealized to the alterego ones.

Religion is both a solitary experience and a communal experience, and both aspects to my mind are extremely important. We have talked up to now about the solitary aspects of religion. For example, you will remember I talked about the most destructive experience of an adult in this century, let us say, to be exterminated or to face extermination. You know why I am stressing the word *extermination*? Because of the dehumanizing attitude. It isn't being killed. To be killed in battle is glorious or was glorious to some people—an uplifting experience, to have lived and died for a great cause, courageously fighting, resisting evil or for whatever crazy goals may now seem to us of the Children's Crusades or aberrations, let us say, of religious goals as there were in the Middle Ages. Yet at that time it was an uplifting experience, and who are we to judge? Certainly to fight tyranny and to be killed in the process by somebody who hates you and opposes you is not a dehumanizing but an uplifting experience. And to be killed by somebody who hates you is better than to be killed like vermin. The people in the concentration camps, especially the Jews, but to some extent also the Slavic people, were exterminated; they were not killed. They were exterminated by people—doctors, for example—who went home after doing away with thousands of people during the day and played coo-coo with their children and loved their wives and who were perfectly normal human beings in the evenings. When you ask him now, "How could you do it?" they would say to us, "Those weren't people we were killing." It is just like somebody who has a job as an exterminator who has killed cockroaches. He comes home and he doesn't mind having killed cockroaches.

But for the victims this is a very different story. To be not even treated as a hated human but simply as a vermin that is being crushed out in the most economical way by poisoning large numbers, that is something that even those who survive would hardly ever recover from. Those who could recover were in many instances those who were capable during their concentration camp stay to hold on to ideals.

There were several groups. There were religious believers: strangely enough such groups even as the Seventh Day Adventists, Orthodox Jews, and of course some high-level Protestants like Dietrich Bonhoeffer. And also people with high and strong political ideals, Old Land communists. These were people who hung onto their ideals. On the basis of the hanging on they could share the last crust of bread with others instead of wolfing it down. And then if by chance, or maybe not so much by chance, they survived and were liberated—you know, sometimes out of ten thousand, twelve, ten, happened to survive as the liberating armies overran those camps—some of those healed without much psychological defect. But the great majority of the others never became truly human anymore. They were like Kafka describes, who have become dehumanized cockroaches, and they feel themselves not worthy of living.

But to go back again, religion is not only an institution that allows you to relate to an idealized other like a god or God, but it is also a communal experience. You feel surrounded by like-minded—you feel surrounded by people with similar needs and similar ways of experiencing and expressing them.

Religion, therefore, has almost always had communal worship as a supportive part. First of all, the preacher, the minister, pastor, is in a sense the symbol, the delegate of God. He is higher up on the pulpit, he preaches to the congregation, he upholds the word of God, he speaks for God. But in addition there is also the sense, the unspoken sense, of many others surrounding you that feel the same thing at the same time and this is a very important supportive experience—the alterego or twinship experience. I would say, therefore, it is not by chance that communal singing plays a role in church: the hymns that everyone knows, into which everyone joins, the well-known hymns, the hymns that go through a seasonal rhythm of church occasions, let us say, from Christmas to Easter, the church year—which, interestingly enough, particularly in the Christian church calendar, is the style of a life, from birth to death to resurrection and then it begins all over again, against, as we all know, the background of seasonal change of winter and spring in which we feel all this and are surrounded by this forever renewing experience.

And then comes the issue of the need to become confirmed, of somebody as it were telling us not only, "I am great and I can lift you up," not only are you surrounded and supported by those like you, but "*You* are supported and special in my eye, the children"—grace.

What is grace? "Man is born broken. He lives by mending. The grace of God is glue," said O'Neill. But it is not by chance that he said so, having had a drug-addicted mother and a very ill-defined sense of acceptance when the mother withdrew from him.

Randall: I've always went to ask you about that because it seems that what you've said about the rudimentary self of the child is that he's not born broken but rather he's born whole.

Kohut: But not if you have a drug-addicted mother. That is the point. You see, his whole life was a life of attempting to mend—that grace had been missing in his early life. One of the most moving modern plays to me is *Long Day's Journey into Night,* in which you see a whole family, two brothers and a father, doing okay. Then all of a sudden they know before it has even happened that mother is upstairs, meaning that she is again back to the drugs. Meaning what? That there is no more grace, no more maternal warmth supporting those men. The men then become enraged and they quarrel with each other and they drink in order to deaden and to put something into them. You are quite right—"The grace of God is glue"—you know, but it's the grace from the beginning. The mending—"he lives by mending"—that we will say only vis-à-vis the failures in the earliest grace that we are supposed to have if we are fairly lucky, and that he was not exposed to because he was very unlucky. And yet maybe all of his genius was needed to mend again through his creativity.

Randall: This is where in your correspondence with Professor Heller you almost celebrate man's fall from grace, because it is then that he always tries to bring about healing and wholeness; it's from this that religion and science emerge.

Kohut: But you see, this is the essence it seems to me, or close to the essence, of human life. It's like my simile with the perfect chord in music. Great music is not just a perfect chord. Great music is always a deviation into dissonance and a complex way of coming again back to the consonance. This is what drives music through the tunes and harmonies until it finally rests or alludes again at the rest of balance. And so we are spurred on by the necessary shortcomings of that early grace—if you want to use the religion term—of acceptance and perfect mirroring, perfect calmness as we are uplifted, and the perfect graspable alterego environment of other human beings. Which child grows up in a perfect milieu? Some scars, some trauma, some shortcomings belong to life.

Randall: It's inevitable.

Kohut: And thank God it is inevitable, because that spurs us on to new ways of solving problems, that gives our sense of initiative something to create. If life were perfect man would never have created religion or art or science.

Randall: That sounds like religion is a deficit issue then again. It arises out of man's limitation.

Kohut: Except that I would not call it deficit. You see, I object to the word "deficit" for the very simple reason that it's a value-laden term, and I don't mean it in a value sense. I think life is movement. It is not a static perfection. And I will consider it not deficit but perfection that human ingenuity, that human responsiveness, is called upon to perform. If we didn't have needs for selfobject support beyond the perfect ones of our immediate family, we wouldn't create institutions like art, science, and religion. I don't call it deficit. I call this the creative response to reality as it is constituted. Not that there are creative tensions in us that want to express something that we experience—I think that enters into the picture. Nevertheless, it seems to me that some need must push us.

Randall: You had said at one time in an interview with Dr. Moss that for you Jesus was not a historical figure. Of course, that flies in the teeth of church people throughout the years who have talked about the incarnate Christ, that he was a very real person. Can you say some more about that?

Kohut: I think what I meant was this: I don't mean to say that Jesus was not a historical figure in a certain sense; but in the sense in which Jesus is important, significant, he was not a historical figure. The search for the historical Christ, like Schweitzer's search for the historical Jesus, that's fine and will be interesting scientifically, perhaps, if it is done well. But it will do nothing, it seems to me, to explain the significance for Western culture of the Jesus Christ figure that was *created* by man, that clustered around a real man and a real event. That is the significance of Christianity, which, of course, has changed tremendously and is continuously changing.

What are the struggles of the Reformation, for instance? The struggles of the Reformation mean that the Reformation, for whatever other things fed into it, had an overriding philosophical and intrinsically religion meaning. I don't mean to say that it hasn't got political and economical and all kinds of other factors. But you know, so much of science is explaining things away and I think good science does not do that. It isn't to explain things away; it's to explain things. The Reformation was man reexamining himself away from what had become empty ritual, away from what had become mercenary—the buying of indulgences—to a trend again to purify values, to purify the individual's relationship to his God, to live up to his God, to facing God, rather than, let us say, the more easy-going mercenary type of religion that Catholicism at the point had become. I don't mean that Catholicism at its best cannot be a marvelous construction and a marvelous institution. Catholicism has the one great virtue: that it consciously addresses itself to different people in different levels. This appeals to people on different levels. I think on the whole the Reformation tried to address itself to the highest tasks that religion can impose on people and that people can live up to. Therefore it may have less appeal to masses, let us say.

Randall: Would you say, then, when you talk about man who needs to be uplifted by higher value, that this religious response of man is a primary human response?

Kohut: I can't answer that. It's obvious so far as we know that no human group has ever been religion-less, so it speaks for this being a very basic trend in human beings. But so also has no human group ever been without some kind of science and some kind of art. Those seem to me the three branches of human activity that are always present.

Randall: Sometimes you include philosophy. Is that not a part of the triumvirate of religion, art, and science?

Kohut: Philosophy stands with one foot in religion and one foot in science. It's a difficult thing, particularly nowadays, where philosophy becomes very frequently a philosophy of science or epistemology, the investigation of the methods of thought and thinking—then it becomes more scientific.

Randall: But in any case you don't usually find cultural groups without some form of science and art and religion.

Kohut: I would think so.

Randall: But I remember in a letter that you once wrote in 1976 [see *The Search for the Self*, 2:905–7]—it must have been to a pastor or a theologian—you said that unless you could find in the reconstruction of early experiences some religious orientation, it would be difficult to say that religion is a primary human experience.

Kohut: Well, I don't remember that letter at all, but I must say a similar thought at this moment crossed my mind. What are the precursors of religion? I would think that—and this doesn't speak against the significance of religion or science or art—that at its best religion is a creation of man's *mature* mind, and, therefore, I dislike—perhaps that is what sort of stymied me—the word "primary." You know, primary means inborn, given, present, as it were, by inherited factors, in the genes. I don't think it is anything like that. In that sense it isn't "primary." Let's be satisfied saying that it is *basic,* created by all human beings; that it belongs and it is different from the scientific attitude of Freud's *The Future of an Illusion;* that it belongs to the highest achievement of the human mind, quite equal in its value and complexity and expression of the depth of man to art and to science.

    I have great respect for religion. But as I said from the very beginning, there's religion and *religion.* As far as I'm concerned, there is no interest for myself in any ironclad mythological beliefs. But communal worship, the uplifting effects of communal worship, man's organization around stable religious institutions—all this is considered to be quite valuable. They can lead to and have led to ludicrous abuses. That people who are in religion and carriers of religion have been as cowardly as the rest of us, you know, that have played up to the powers that be rather than courageously stood up for beliefs—that I would not doubt. But, on the other hand, there've been very many people who have courageously stood up with the aid of religion.

Randall: You talk about people who have stood up courageously with the aid of religion, and about people being uplifted by their values and by meanings. What is it that determines their status, Dr. Kohut? If we go back to our first interview, what determines that Churchill's high meanings and visions are more correct than Hitler's? What makes the "blueprint," as you call it, laid down in a person's self, more acceptable or valuable or meaningful than the blueprint of another?

Kohut: In the last analysis we come without any question to certain axiomatic beliefs in what *we* value as the highest value. Can such beliefs be substantiated and in any way correspond, let us say, to verification in science? I think no. The point is that to me it is axiomatic that man wants to maintain the variety of human experience, that man wants to maintain human life and cultured human life as he has reached it and known it and wants to go beyond it. When you compare Churchill and Hitler you are comparing not just two people—that's not the issue at all. They have something in common, these two people, namely that they could inspire large groups of people to follow them. But what were the ideals that inspired *them*? The Hitlerian ideal is essentially one that one might call "vulgarized Darwinism": that it is a superior race, that it's a good thing for the superior races to eradicate the inferior races, that that's the way the cookie crumbles, that's the way the world goes, and it happens to be that the German race was the best one in the world and that he was the best among the German race. So, therefore, everything goes. It's a certain unanswerable, as I said, vulgarization of Darwinism.

So why do I say "vulgarization"? I don't know what Darwin himself believed. It may very well have been that Darwin believed in something on that order, you know, that he believed, maybe, that the Anglo-Saxon race—everyone always believes his own is the peak—was the one that was the peak of culture and therefore the peak of mankind and therefore had the right to subdue the Indians and colonize people, et cetera, et cetera. Now the question is that even if you apply Darwinism to human relationships, which is a very bad exportation to make, but even if you do that, you could argue quite differently. You could argue that maybe the survival of the human species depends on the capacity to *subdue* that hatred against each other and to be capable to be respectful toward each other, to accept the variety of human expressiveness, and that we will have much more of a chance to survive than by, you know, exterminating each other and being contemptuous of each other.

But apart from that fact, if we examine these arrogant and extreme attitudes of self-confidence, behind them almost always are tremendous needs to be accepted and the enormous doubts in one's self. I mean, as far as the prehistory of the Nazis are concerned, I could quote you chapter and verse on how the German nation—a very cultured, in many ways a brilliant nation—could fall prey to this kind of aberration; because everything that had sustained them broke down during the period between the wars: the pride in the army disappeared, the stabilized belief in their emperor disappeared, religion was undermined, the money-earning capacities of the breadwinners in the family were nil because of the enormous unemployment—there was loss of the monetary value by this inflation which is nothing like our inflation, although that is demoralizing too, but inflation that made money essentially and savings totally valueless—and the contempt that they felt about themselves. And then comes a man who says, "No. You are not the worst. You are the best!" And he said that with utter conviction and then people are perfectly willing to die for it, like they are for Reverend Jones. I mean it is the same phenomena as it is for Reverend Moon.

But there you have to examine who are the flocks, the children, who are abandoned. Who are those presidential murderers or potential murderers? Who are those drifters that go around with guns and want to shoot somebody? Examine what happened to them and why the parents don't even know where they are, the total lack of interest in them. They then find either some crazy idea of shooting somebody big that puts them into the limelight, or they find the religion like the Moonies, the Reverend Jones, who will uplift them, or they become neo-Nazis, and say they belong to the master race, and are not only not neglected but just the opposite—they are the best. Then they join into this kind of leader.

The Western people were very loath to rise against this; they were paralyzed to the danger. But finally they found this rallying point in Churchill who was unafraid, who upheld Western ideals ands Western traditions, and as such became a rallying point for what I happen to believe is good and what you happen to believe is good.

But these are values that you must take as axioms. We happen to have values of mutual support, values of mutual respect, values of the tolerance for the variety of human beings and human existences. Those are the things, and they are symbolized in Western religions by, let us say, by a superfamily family imagery of a God who loves *all* varieties of human beings, and they all bask in his grace, and they all are united in their worship of him, and they are all reflected as it were by him and feel alive. They look up to the same ideal, they are uplifted by the same ideal, something of that order. This is an extremely important issue, but you can—I think most of us nowadays are capable of doing this—realize that there are a variety of other experiences that one can treat with respect, that one must extend one's empathy to and at least begin to build a bridge of understanding before one can meaningfully dialogue and talk.

Randall: Speaking about the dialogue and talk, at our first meeting you talked about how it had to be a two-way street in the dialogue between religion and depth psychology, that religion had to listen to what self psychology in particular had to say and the other way around as well. Can you think of some particular issues that religion and depth psychology can mutually address, where both can contribute, not just listen; some fruitful junctures where they can share their understandings and insights?

Kohut: Yes. At least I can outline the samples. Let's take for example just a simple thing as the pastoral counselor. You don't have to know any more. You have learned a great deal from self psychology, obviously, so that's clearly the one-way street.

Or let us take for example such a thing as the visitation of the sick and the dying, which is an aspect of the minister's job in most churches, grasping from self psychology, as I just before told you, how one relates to a person, to give him a sense of the meaningfulness of death, of his being an example, or the ever-returning new creativeness of life going on, or the fullness of the life that is now fading away and how gratifying it must be, like at the end of a busy and fruitful day, to go to sleep. I mean, there are a variety of ways in which a minister or pastoral counselor or whoever it is who visits a dying member of a congregation or a very ill member can be of help. And this help can be increased by the insights of self psychology, that is, of the needs of the self—that even a fading self can be a very strong and proud self and that it can be supported. And the same is true in family crises and what have you. So there are numerous ways, I am sure.

Let's think, for instance, about the meaning of worship, of the dangers to which a minister is exposed by his elevated position, you know, by the arrogance that may get filtered into him, by the loss of the responsibility of the parental position vis-à-vis his flock. You know, the Catholic church with its celibacy rule is, to my mind, an exaggerated extreme of something that basically is very sound. It is a position—priest, minister, pastor—toward his congregation, is a position that in some essentials is like the position of parents to children. It has nothing to do with the age. The children may be twice as old as the parents. By the way, exactly the same is true for the psychiatrist, the psychotherapist, the psychoanalyst. There is something intergenerational about this position. Therefore it does in some important ways exclude sexual gratification. A minister who is promiscuous with the women of his congregation is an utter failure to my mind. It is incest, in the same way as if a father would sleep with or fondle his daughter sexually. That doesn't mean that a minister can't marry somebody in his flock, but then, you know, this is the one exception that is a different relationship. But on the whole the minister's relationship with his flock is not a sexual interrelationship. The minister is the ideal who, on the whole, watches over and provides a certain structure to the congregation. I know perfectly well that parishioners marry one another, and that parishioners may have affairs with each other, and that there are young adult groups for meeting others and getting involved. That's fine so long as it is organized. But when it becomes orgiastic, when limits of decency as it were are not maintained, I think it weakens the religious organization.

I'm not an old foggy. I'm all for freedom and openness about sex. But one should realize the religious institution is essentially an uplifting one and serves a particular purpose of the maintenance of the self. So all these are things, and I by no means am rigid about them. The more secure one feels the more freedom one can allow one's self. There is nothing wrong with freedom in terms of bodily closeness and bodily enjoyment, even within the framework of a congregation. But on the whole this is not what the essence of religion is. Otherwise it becomes, as it were, a club, and it loses the essence and the support that religion is to give to people. Who needs religion if it's no more than a way of finding a partner to get married to or to go out with. Some people I suppose go to church to some extent for that purpose, and I wouldn't call them evil or anything else, but this is not what religion in essence is all about. So those are issues that I believe religion can learn from self psychology and from the inside state of the self.

But how about the other way around? Can we learn something from religion? I would say, sight unseen, a lot. How could it be otherwise? Religion is much older that psychiatry. Religion has been established much longer than psychoanalysis. Religion has insights into the needs of human beings, not scientifically organized the way we do, but they still are something from which one can learn. The mere phenomenon of religiosity and how people react in their needs toward institutionalized religion is something from which we ought to take cues. What does it do for people? I'm not a do-gooder basically, and I'm not a sentimentalist basically. I don't spout words like "love" and "curing through love," because I don't believe one cures through love, at least not in any reliable way, and not in any enduring way.

But I do know one thing. When somebody comes to me with an illness, a psychological illness, and I tell him my method is such and such, it might go on for a long time, you will talk and I will listen, I know that my saying this has already set up a very, very important curative framework. It is not only that I will make the unconscious conscious. It is not only that I'll gradually acquaint him with conflicts that he didn't know he had, or needs that he did not know he had, the needs of the self, for instance, for reverberation or acclaim or approval or whatnot, that he therefore after knowing it can provide for himself more effectively. There's also something else. Merely to be in an atmosphere in which somebody else says, "I will pay attention to you, concentratedly, so many times a week, for endless times, until we feel we have had enough," that alone is curative in a way. Not sufficiently so, but it is not a neutral situation. To be reliably in the center of somebody else's attention is an extremely important event, particularly for people who have not had enough of that when they were children.

I don't mean to say that every form of psychopathology is that way. There may be children that were over stimulated. They had too much attention, too much intrusiveness from their parents, that they could never be alone and develop undisturbed by another person's presence. But you will soon learn that when you listen to such a person that he wants to be left alone and not to be disturbed. He, too, is being understood and listened to in his particular needs.

Of course in the modern world it is my conviction, as you know, that the needs of the unresponded to self are paramount, rather than the needs of the conflicted self. I think that we can learn a great deal of what successful religion has done for people, and has done without enslaving them and without leading them astray, but, as it were, stimulating what is potentially the best in them.

I don't think that religion can or should basically instill new values and goals in people. I think people have their values and goals. I don't mean to say that the Sunday sermon shouldn't contain an outspoken opinion about this, that and the other. But still, that is the man in the minister who wrote that. The main thing is that he is up to something higher than the immediate advantage, that he is up to supporting something that is strong in the person that he alone could not perhaps support. He may even disagree with the minister and feel uplifted, or may not understand what the minister said and feel uplifted. That is not anything that science can give to man. That is not anything that art can give to man.

Randall: That's very interesting to hear you say that because I was going to ask if an artist interviewed you next week would you simply, in one way or another, say the same things to him about art that you are saying to me about religion?

Kohut: I don't think so. You see, neither art nor science are as deeply action related as is religion. In the highest sense of the word religion adds to man's courageousness, to his willingness to take risks, to his willingness to live for something beyond his paralogical existence. I have been very interested in and have written a good deal about it, but it has not been published yet, although an historian is cooperating with me to publish these unpublished historical asides that I have alluded to a number of time in my writings. I became interested in those very few lonely resisters to Nazi tyranny, which took an *enormous* amount of courage to be. And almost all of them, almost all of them, had some religious beliefs that supported them. There was a lonely farmer in Austria by the name of Yagersteter who had a religious inspiring dream before he became a resister, in which God spoke to him. But he was not hallucinating; he was not psychotic. There were the brothers and sisters Scholl in Munich; they were supported by religious or religious-like beliefs. And there were others. I don't demean that. Many of the other very bright and intellectual people who knew things were wrong that were going on did not have the courage, because life was more important to them than living up to the ideal. Now whether there are other means of supporting ideals and courageous action, I don't know. Obviously there are. There's patriotism that has sustained people. There's simply inspiring human leaders. All this is true. But these are things that are more related to short-term goals and advantages, where religion in a sense is a carrier of long-term values. And to my mind I hope and I trust that the best in religion will support what I consider to be the best of the values of man—that is, the mutual support of man toward the maintenance of man's life at its best and its further development.

Randall: Dr. Kohut, you've talked and written often about how the psychology of the self is also action oriented in its attempt to support as well as structure some of the higher meanings of life. How does that differ from religion which tries to do this?

Kohut: Well, self psychology is not a cultural institution. Self psychology is and should be and will remain a science. In other words, we do not aspire to uplift people via self psychology, although some people are uplifted by it.

Randall: They certainly are.

Kohut: I know. Some people are uplifted by it, but that doesn't mean that this is the essence of it.

Randall: That must be why you sometimes call it a quasi religion.

Kohu: Alright. I don't remember that I said that. But I think self psychology is a branch of psychology, and it explains in terms of people with self defects, is capable of isolating those self defects in a course of therapy that is informed by self psychological insights, and helps to heal the self, and that's a different story. Religion cannot, as a cultural institution, cure a person with serious self defects. It can, however, uplift people and maintain people in their usual swings of ups and downs of self-esteem and courage and powers and self-exertion.

What is courage? You know, this is a very important question that we need to ask ourselves. I think it is simply best explained as a function of the strength of the self, of the strength and cohesiveness of the self; that is, of a self that knows where it is aiming and to whom biological survival under extreme circumstances is less important than the program that it wants to fulfill. It was a beautiful, beautiful dream that Sophie Scholl had on the night before her execution. I've mentioned the Scholl's before. They were young resisters in Munich against the Nazis, a group of people: the brothers and sisters Scholl and a few others that went with them. They didn't do anything so great, you know, really, except that knowing the enormous pressures on them from all sides, it is incredible what they did. They had printing presses and they distributed handbills at the university and they argued against the Nazi, and they argued against the policies of the Nazis, and they were caught finally and executed.

But Sophie Scholl, who was, I think, twenty-one at the time, or twenty, or something like that, had this dream during the night before she was executed. She had a cellmate and told the cellmate the dream or wrote it down and the cellmate lived, who was not involved in that conspiracy. The dream was that she had a baby in her hand and that she was walking up a very steep hill. Then all of sudden an abyss opened from earth, there was a cleft in the ground, and she began to fall. But as she fell she quickly put the baby on the other side—and she disappeared. And the cellmate asked, "Now what does that mean? Why did you dream that?" And she said, "Don't you understand? That's so clear." So what was it? She said, "Well, I will die tomorrow, but the baby, that's my ideals, that will live on, and I don't mind dying so long as that baby lives on." And she was watched during the whole day. She was executed four or five in the afternoon, they were all beheaded, and she was in marvelous shape—not anxious, calm; not pale, but pink cheeked and with full lips—a person having what we would call *narcissistic balance*. Her self was secure.

These were no psychotic kids. Her brother was a medical student in Munich and from time to time had to go to the front to serve several weeks every year on the Russian front. Once the train stopped somewhere in the middle of nowhere in Poland and he saw a bunch of women working in the fields with the Star of David on their backs. They were Jewish girls. And he saw a particularly beautiful one, black hair, working close to the train. And so he in his uniform—the train was stopped—jumped out and full of pity for these poor girls gave her his rations. She saw that he was what she considered a Nazi soldier and she contemptuously threw it at his feet. So he picked it up and walked back to the train. But then he felt better of it and he went to the field and picked one flower and he went back to her and put the flower at her feet and then walked back to the train. And when the train went into motion he saw her with the flower in her hair waving at him. I mean, the subtlety of this man's empathy for what another human being needed was marvelous. It was obviously not psychotic. And the same was true for Yagersteter as with the dream, the sense of humor that he had up to the moment in which he was executed. There is no question about these people being deeply human people.

Randall: Talking about them, Dr. Kohut, what is it that lays down that *blue print* that you often write about? How does it happen that these people have that kind of *blue print*, not just a consolidation of the self, but that kind of project?

Kohut: You see, I would probably assume that regardless of what the content is of our later goals in life—they can be varied, enormously varied, from person to person, from culture to culture—and yet there is something that all of us have alike, whether we are Chinese or Tibetans or Russians or aborigines in the Australian bush or inhabitants of Manhattan. We are surrounded from early on by a responsive human environment. And it is this earliest experience that in one form or another goes on and on and on, gradually translates into complex institutions, like science that takes care of your body, and art that provides you with beauty, and religion that provides you with communal singing and uplifting ideals. However complexingly varied these things may become later—obviously the tom toms of aborigines are different from a Beethoven quartet—and yet in essence they have something that reverberates the early responsiveness to us. We are in a human, understanding environment and the *break* is only where you have, let us say, a psychotic parent or where you may suddenly live in a psychotic culture.

Now it is true that for those that were accepted by Hitler it was not psychotic, but for those who were not, there was suddenly a real break. It was again the psychotic mother of early life—human beings not just censuring you, not just saying to have to live this way or that, but suddenly not accepting you as human anymore. Anybody that can do that to another human, there is something seriously wrong. That conviction I have. Which is very different from killing. If you fight you have to kill, for a goal, but once you have won you aren't interested in killing anymore. That is different from exterminating. There is the old question, "Is there progress in history? Is history meaningful?" My own feelings is always that man is always trying to find institutions that create, on the one hand, sufficient stability, but, on the other hand, sufficient openness to allow for new creative solutions. It must be both However good a dictator may be, however perfect the goals of a dictator may be, it's stifling. However imperfect freedoms are, they challenge us to find solutions in the very friction of the disorder.

So we come back again to what you asked me much earlier, you know: is it a defect issue? And I would say, no, this is not a defect. That is the creativeness that needs to be at stake. Just to have it imposed on us, perfection, is never enough. There must be this freedom of suffering and trying to relieve it. And no childhood can be perfect, but it's a difference between an occasionally impatient and overtired mother and father, and an occasionally brutality, and the lonesomeness from the stonewall of a mother who can never understand what her children are all about.

Randall: Dr Kohut, you've been very gracious with your time and I thank you a lot for that and for what you've offered.

8

Getting Something from Kohut's Perspective on Religion

IN THIS FINAL CHAPTER, we will respond to the previous interviews between Randall and Kohut, as well as offer some additional reflections on Kohut's value for understanding the psychological functions of religion. While the entire chapter represents our combined and united work, we will respond individually to these issues. We believe this will provide the reader with a broader and more comprehensive analysis of Kohut's potential as a dialogue partner with religion. Thus, Randall's reflections will be followed by Cooper's.

RANDALL'S RESPONSE TO THE INTERVIEWS

We are pragmatists. We wrote this book convinced that Kohut's self psychology perspective offers concrete benefits for the life of ministry. Whether thinking about old ideas in new ways, or practicing old behaviors in altered ways, Kohut's work is a helpmate. At least we hope you are experiencing that.

But are there pragmatic benefits from grasping that Kohut is also a soulmate? Does Kohut's defense of religion, even his affirmation of religion, contribute anything to a person whose religious life is already firm and foundational? What's in it for the believer? Indeed, what's in it for the semi-believer, or the seeker, or that person whose religious life has shriveled up? We suggest three contributions.

First, religion today is beleaguered by new critics. Some are from the evolutionary field; others from other fields. Kohut provides a potent rebuttal to today's critics through his rebuttal of the all-time arch-critic of religion—Sigmund Freud. Second, Kohut provides a perspective on how religion functions that illuminates both its indispensable role and its fundamental nature. Third, Kohut establishes groundwork for the interfacing and cooperating of religion and science (particularly psychology) as different but equal partners in the effort to bring grace to injured selves. We'll briefly celebrate these three.

Defending Religion

In the above interviews, Kohut adamantly rebuts Freud's approach to religion. Freud's cardinal mistake was attempting to evaluate religion as a science. Operating from the axiomatic value that humankind should live by thoughts corresponding to reality (as science does), Freud declared that religious beliefs were fantasies and religious experiences were illusions. Furthermore, Freud considered these religious fantasies and illusions as manifestations of the infantile state of psychological development, particular of the primitive state of narcissism. Inasmuch as Freud's psychoanalytic aim was to move people beyond infantile drives and fantasy wishes, he espoused the relinquishment of religion for a healthier view of reality. This is putting it mildly, of course. There were considerable amounts of belittling, castigating narcissistic rage directed toward religion by Freud and some of his followers.

Throughout his life, Kohut was very appreciative of Freud's work. He could, however, healthily idealize Freud without accepting everything Freud postulated. That applied particularly to religion. In the first place, Kohut was not committed to Freud's axiomatic value of "correspondence with reality." Instead, he was committed to the axiomatic value of "consolidation of the self." Strengthening the self of individuals rather than correcting their distorted thoughts was Kohut's main aim. It was erroneous, therefore, for Freud to apply scientific cognition to religion, because this is not what "true religion" is all about.[1]

Freud was only correct in deploring religion, Kohut said, when religion *itself* tries to be science. Consequently, Kohut exposed both Freud's error and the error of some religious groups. Kohut refuted any effort to reduce religion to inner fantasy or to reduce religion to an outer reality. Religion is not simply the fantasy-filled psychological world of individuals; nor is it the non-psychological world of fact and subject-object reality. In short, religion is not science and should not be judged as science (Freud); nor should religion consider itself the same as fact-filled science (some religious groups).

In the second place, since Kohut's primary value was consolidation of the self, he spoke positively about how illusions and the work of imagination can be extremely helpful to people as they struggle to maintain their self cohesion. Rather than ridicule religion as infantile fantasy, Kohut authenticated the vital role of religious thoughts and beliefs couched in images beyond logical thought that serve the life-saving task of lifting up and sustaining the selves of individuals and groups. Just like Kohut took Freud's drive theory and folded it into his self psychology, so he took Freud's views on fantasy and folded them into his self psychology perspective. Seen from this viewpoint, what appears to be regressive religious fantasies and illusions can be, indeed, positive resources protecting and restoring the threatened cohesion of persons and groups.

In the third place, rather than see religion as a symptom of individuals and groups stuck in the immature, narcissistic stage of development, Kohut stressed that healthy religion is a product of the man's "mature" mind.[2] Religion does have roots in early self experiences, but religion *per se* is a form of "transformed narcissism," of narcissistic inclinations raised to the highest level of human expression. Kohut certainly understood how some expressions of religion *are* manifestations of regressive narcissism (just as he understood how certain reactions in psychoanalysis as a discipline were expressions of archaic narcissistic needs and yearnings). But such "clinical" expressions of religious behavior should not to be taken as legitimate reasons for condemning religion itself.[3]

Many religious individuals and groups feel threatened by current attacks on their religious faith and institutions, and understandably so. But part of living as cohesive selves is the ability not only to "stand strong" against criticism but even to "stand receptive" to criticism—to learn what one can from one's critics. Kohut provides intellectual and moral support in religion's beleaguered effort to be an uplifting voice for lives constantly in need of grace.

Illuminating Religion

Kohut illuminates religion in two ways: by shinning elevating light on its cultural significance and by shinning revealing light on its fundamental nature. In regard to the first, Freud considered the cultural structure of religion as simply the individual's religious fantasy writ large. Religion in its corporate or institutional state was a transference of infantile fantasy wishes into cultural forms. Religion was "cultural transference," and since, from a classical psychoanalytic perspective, all transferences were to be relinquished in favor of correspondence with reality, religion as a cultural transference should also be exposed and relinquished.

For Kohut, however, religion was not "cultural transference" but a "great cultural selfobject." He had talked about "cultural selfobjects" in the past, referring to great heroes, inspiring leaders, who people of a culture attached to as mirroring, idealized, or alterego selfobjects. But here in these interviews Kohut for the first time fully illuminates a higher level of cultural selfobjects. He calls them "great cultural selfobjects." These are the seminal and indispensable cultural selfobject supports of all human life, and there are only three: science, art, and religion.

Kohut does not believe that religion has a divine origin. Religion, like art and science, is a creation of the human mind, a creative expression of the self that is, in certain ways, still ongoing.[4] But religion is also something that meets the self, that functions in human life as a "great cultural selfobject." For Kohut religion is "a powerful and meaningful and valuable force in human life."[5] As a valued force it has a specific supportive function: "the holding together, the strengthening, the harmonizing of man's self in general."[6] In this work of lifting up and sustain the self of persons and groups religion is indispensable. Human survival depends upon its supportive selfobject function. Indeed, religion's indispensable work cannot be done by other sources, cannot be done by any cultural selfobject or any other great cultural selfobjects.[7] When other human endeavors attempt to usurp or mimic religion's unique function, then it endangers its own self. For example, Kohut saw religious overtones begin to surface in classical psychoanalysis. Those covert religious traits threatened the progress of the analytic movement.

From observing how religion can seep into other domains, and from observing that no recorded culture has been without religion, and from analyzing religion as an indispensable great cultural selfobject, Kohut concludes, "I believe . . . that seen in the broadest possible way, no one can do or does do without religion, in one form or another."[8]

Late in the second interview Randall tested the waters with Kohut, asking, in essence, if religion was "primary," if it was an innate part of human nature. Kohut quickly caught the gist of the question and defused it. He did not like the term "primary," he said, and he did not like to reduce religion to something "given," such as in the genes. That would detract from understanding the function of religion as a "great cultural selfobject." The highest affirmation/description he could offer was to declare that religion belongs to the highest achievement of the human mind, that it is present in all life, that it has an indispensable and unique function, and that it is equal in value and complexity and expression of the depth of man to art and to science.[9]

To the religious believer this illuminating perspective can be reinforcement for what they already know. For those who seek religion, it offers the vision that what they seek is valuable, and that, indeed, it is there to be found. To the semi-believer or to the one whose religious faith has shriveled, Kohut's perspective encourages at least a hearty embrace of religion for the indispensable support it offers human selves on many different levels.[10] One may no longer believe, but one can still celebrate the magnificent function of religion as a "great cultural selfobject."

Kohut also illuminates the fundamental structure of religion. Let's begin by noting that psychological and religious thought is dominated by subject-object thinking. For much of psychology this is a goal. Reaching the subject-object state means: (1) having reached the fullness of psychological development (an individual/subject as an independent entity in interactions with others/objects as independent entities); and (2) having reached the capacity to view life objectively (living from a "correspondence with reality" orientation).

For much of theology, the subject-object reality has been a problem. If life is basically subject-object reality, where I, as subject, am basically separate from others, as objects, then this poses the problem of how to overcome this essential estrangement in human life, especially in the relationship between humankind and God.[11]

Kohut transformed much of psychological thought when he showed that subject-object life is not primary. The psychological bedrock of life is the self-selfobject relationship. The starting point for understanding individuals and groups is not subject-object separation; the starting point is self-selfobject togetherness.

This can also give new direction for religious thinking. For Kohut, once again, the basic unit of human experience and human reality is the self-selfobject relationship. A self is not a separate entity supported by impersonal selfobject functions; nor are selfobjects separate entities ready for use by various selves. A self and its selfobjects in-dwell, constitute each other. There *are* subject-object human interactions, of course, existing at the same time as self-selfobject relationships, but the self-selfobject matrix is the psychological bedrock of human reality. It is also, as we have discussed, the primary unit for observing and understanding and preserving human selves.

Therefore, the starting point for working with disordered relationships within the church is not to see them as rooted in an essential estrangement based in our innate subject-object status. The starting point instead is acknowledging the essential connected of people based upon the bedrock of our self-selfobject relating. Pastoral care work in churches focuses most productively not on trying to "build bridges" between independent, subject-object selves (although this can be helpful), but on repairing and transforming the capacity to live maturely one's ongoing self-selfobject life, where one's selfobjects are both extensions of the self and the primary supports and substance of the self. Stated informally, we are all in it together, connected from the beginning and forever. There is no "bailing out," no "going it alone" no matter how far away we travel or how long we are gone. Restoration, grace, occurs through nurturing this elemental self-selfobject way of being in the world as best as we can.

Similarly, the starting point for contemplating one's relationship with God can be the self-selfobject reality. Whether one has "always believed in God," or "found God for the first time," or was "always vaguely aware there was a higher power," the basic experience of that connection between self and God/higher power is a self-selfobject relationship. God (whether image, thought, or sensation) is an extension of the self (its selfobject), while that selfobject God also constitutes the experiencing self. When Jesus said to his disciples, "I am in you and you are in me," he was expressing the central experience, and holiness, of the self-selfobject relationship. Self and selfobject are "in" each other; they constitute each other.

Grasping this reality, religion can begin to reformulate thoughts about the relationship between the self and God. Its former aim at overcoming estrangement can change. The altered aim can become one of understanding, contemplating, enjoying, and benefiting from the rich indwelling of self-self and self-God in life's original, basic, bedrock self-selfobject reality.

While Kohut does not explicitly say it this way, what he wants to convey is that *religious experience is selfobject experience.* An individual's religious experience/relationship with, for example, God, Jesus, a pastor, the sacraments, an individual church, the wider Church, or even with the idea of "religion" itself, is basically a selfobject experience/relationship. Whatever the focus of one's religious attachment may be, that attachment is a selfobject attachment.

Not all selfobject experiences are religious experiences, although some may try to claim differently. Conversely, not all contemplation of religion is selfobject experience. One can study religion as an "object" in a subject-object way, being interested in religion, maybe even making a living as a religious scholar, but not psychologically invested in religion. Similarly, attempting to vicariously experience the religious experiences of others is not selfobject experience. But when an individual becomes self-invested in faith figures or rituals or ideas, then this investment, this religious experience, is basically a selfobject experience. Those figures, rituals, and ideas become mirroring, idealized, or alterego supporters, inspirers, and protectors of the self's psychological world. They serve, with varying degrees of importance, as selfobjects for the self's cohesion and esteem.

This applies even when a person is harshly critical of religion. Narcissistic rage against religion emanates from a person's response to religion as an entity (selfobject) that has gravely disturbed the cohesion of the person's self in some way. This negative "religious experience" is itself selfobject experience. The person is not responding to religion, religious figures, or religious ideas as "objects" that the self can more coolly evaluate and perhaps reject. Instead, religion, religious figures, or religious ideas are infuriating irritants in the narcissistic world of the self that must be demolished to some degree. In short, they are selfobjects eliciting narcissistic rage.

From this perspective on religious experience as selfobject experience we can expand on Kohut's illumination of the nature of religion in two ways. The first has to do with the "domain" of religion; the second has to do with its "origins." Regarding the first, at the moment of religious experience, mild or intense, the subject-object world gives way to a certain degree. The self-selfobject matrix moves from psychological depth closer to conscious experience as one senses that one's self and the object of one's religious focus have merged, become one. This merger sensation may last only a few seconds, or it may be a semi-continuous experience as individuals daily walk with God or hold the hand of Jesus in nearly every situation.

In those moments of religious experience, "religion" is neither an "external" nor an "internal" reality; neither a "great cultural selfobject" nor a self-creation of the highest order. Instead, religion here is a self-selfobject reality. It is in this experiential/psychological domain that religion exists and has its fundamental reality. It is to this domain that a psychology of religion or phenomenology of religion or even a sociology of religion can begin to find its object of inquiry.

Second, while Kohut intentionally avoids interpretations about religion's origin (expect to say that it is as an expression of the self), it is possible to use Kohut's perspective as a thought experimentation regarding religion's origin. Religious experience, we have posited, is selfobject experience. Religion, therefore, perhaps did not spring from individual fantasy wishes writ large, or as a power ploy by control-seeking individuals, or from an intrinsic "given" within human nature. Instead, religion may have arisen from the general necessity of every self to exist in a matrix of self-selfobject relationship. More specifically, religion may have originated from the healthy need of selves to consolidate their selves through connecting with a matrix of selfobjects with especially powerful mirroring, idealized, and alterego capacities. This, of course, is what we plainly see in every day religious life. This *is* how religion seems to function. And perhaps what *is* is also *why* the *is* came to be. At the psychological bedrock of life is the self-selfobject matrix, that essential nucleus that has as its central life aim the consolidation of the self. Religion is an expression of that matrix and a powerful contributor to that aim, and may have arisen to serve that deep psychological life-orientation.

For religious seekers, or for those religiously weak, the illuminating light Kohut sheds on the fundamental nature of religion can be motivating. The struggle is not to overcome one's estrangement from God, for example. Instead, the effort is to make one's self receptive to God as selfobject, *to which the self is naturally receptive in its general need for selfobject supports, and particularly receptive in its yearning for powerful selfobjects.* We may not be "made" for God, but each person is made needful of and receptive to ultimate selfobjects.

Conjoining Religion

Kohut always had an abiding interest in the humanities, of which religion is a part. They were an enjoyable part of his growing up and contributed permanently to his intellect. As Kohut became focused later in life on the importance of encompassing empathy for the needs of selves, and especially on the axiomatic value of contributing to the emotional, biological, and spiritual well-being of selves, his embrace of the humanities became pragmatically crucial. Human survival required all the buttressing of value and meaning that is possible, and that must also come, stressed Kohut, from resources "beyond the psychoanalytic circle."

It was for this basic reason that Kohut showed great interest in meeting with Robert Randall. He wanted not only to help religion begin to understanding its selfobject function as a "great cultural selfobject" but also to further his message that those in the psychology field needed to learn from religion and to appreciate the importance of religion for the survival of humanity. It was a "two-way street," Kohut would adamantly state. In other places Randall has spelled out the ways in which this two-way conjoining of religion and psychology can begin to happen when narcissistic obstacles are overcome and healthy selfobject relationships are formed between these two endeavors.[12] What we want to stress here, however, is the concerted effort of Kohut to extend his hand of colleagueship to other healing approaches outside the self psychology circle, and to urge them to join hands with each other and with self psychology until a broad, empathic circle is formed in which healing endeavors learn from each other in their mutual commitment to the preservation of humanity.

Those in the religious circle can take this as more than an invitation to join in conversation with "elite" secular endeavors (psychology, psychoanalysis, science, for example). Instead, it is Kohut's welcome and embrace of the religious circle as an esteemed, equal partner both in itself and as a contributor to the healing grace so desperately needed by injured selves.

It is the authors' assessment that those in the religious circle are much more receptive to Kohut's welcome than those in the psychology circle are to welcoming religion. But this has always been the case historically. Kohut has tried to change this, not passively but persistently. May those who have ears hear.

COOPER'S RESPONSE TO THE INTERVIEWS

Kohut is interested in religion primarily because he is interested in human beings. In other words, Kohut's central concern is building up and supporting the cohesion of the self so that it has a possibility of achieving its potential. To say that Kohut takes an anthropological approach to the study of religion is to put it mildly. For instance, Kohut does not seem to raise questions about the ontological status of various religious claims, nor does he express an epistemological curiosity about religion's foundations. It seems enough for him that healthy or "true" religion serves to build up and support humanity's vocation. Religion accomplishes this primarily through its "uplifting" capacities. It addresses humanity's needs for mirroring, idealizing, and a sense of kinship. Believing that the universe is responsive to our own need for significance, that we have a Source for idealization (God), and that we sit in pews with like-minded people all help provide cohesion to our vulnerable and fragile sense of self. Stated another way, religion performs significant selfobject functions. In fact, as a cultural selfobject, religion can inspire us, shore us up, support our most elevated values, and infuse us with a sense of meaning and significance. Religion points toward the ultimate empathic milieu— a context in which our deepest strivings are supported and encouraged by Divine affirmation. A supportive Other invites the emergence of the nuclear program of the self. It is not a stretch to see this inner sense of purpose and direction as the *imago Dei*. Even in the midst of our brokenness, Kohut could see how the grace we claim emanates from God is the glue that holds us together. The anxiety of self fragmentation is accompanied by a Source of divine soothing.

Kohut's notion that a major function of religion is the building up and support of the self will no doubt provoke criticism from some theological corners. Some would quickly counter that the function of religion is to glorify and adore God, to "sing God's praises" in a worshipful manner. Yet perhaps Kohut would challenge the psychological roots of this image of God. For, as we have seen, this image seems dangerously close to a narcissistically injured God who insists upon constant attention, a God who brings humanity into existence primarily because of mirror-hunger. This image of God is somewhat reminiscent of a narcissistically deprived parent who wants children largely out of a profound need for attention and adoration. Here nature is reversed: rather than the parent being there in a supportive way for the child, the child is expected to fill a void within the parent. Seeking a relationship with one's child is quite different than demanding an audience. As we observed in chapter 2, some of our conceptions of the Divine represent a narcissistically deprived God hypersensitive to neglect and inattention. This is a God who is easily offended and prone toward narcissistic rage. While there are limits to Divine-human analogies, it is helpful to realize that just as a healthy parent wants to bring a child into this world out of surplus of love and a desire to nurture, a healthy image of God offers empathic responsiveness and care. The central motive of such an envisioned God is to seek relationships, not to be continually praised.

Religion and Human Needs

Kohut is perhaps most helpful in his dialogue about religion when he identifies the basic needs of individuals throughout their lives and the way in which religion can respond to those needs. Kohut reminds us of the importance of experience-near concepts, and conversely, the problem of experience-distant, highly abstract theological language. While some degree of abstraction is of course necessary (just as it is in Kohut's own theorizing about the self), theological language friendly to the actual experience of people is crucial. One is reminded here of Luther's famous line, "A theologian is born by living, dying, and being damned, not by thinking, reading, or speculating."[13] Kohut helps us understand how grace meets particular human needs, needs that remain with us from birth to death. He helps us move away from a judgmental and distant theology to an experience-near sense of affirmation and acceptance.

Just as self psychologists need to appreciate the positive function of religion in the lives of people, so religious leaders need to grasp the specific psychological functions that religion helps fulfill. As Kohut puts it:

> . . . it is a two-way street and not a one-way street. Not only should self psychologists and psychologists in general appreciate the meaning that religion has in the maintenance of man's self, but, on the other hand, people engaged in religious activities as ministers, as healers within a religious framework, that they too should broaden and deepen their self-understanding about the meaning of their functions. . . . I think they [professionals in the religious field] would come out ahead if they would study our contributions in depth, as you are trying to make them do. That is the value, it seems to me, of your contributions.[14]

This is *not* to suggest that all study of religion should be reduced to an elaboration of how it contributes to the cohesion of the self. But certainly we need to better understand how religion addresses the deep-seated psychological needs of human beings.

Yet again, some theological voices will no doubt object to any no-tion of theology being evaluated in terms of its impact on human fulfill-ment. Neo-orthodoxy, in particular, would strongly resist this emphasis on human experience as crucial for "evaluating" Christian theology. This makes all the more interesting Kohut's affirming comment about hear-ing Karl Barth speak in Rockefeller Chapel at the University of Chicago. This positive remark about Barth is a little ironic, particularly because Kohut's emphasis on the usefulness of religion to help humanity achieve its ambitions would clearly provoke a disapproving word from Barth. For Barth, this is precisely the problem with an anthropological religion. Ultimately, it reduces theology to the psychological needs of humanity. Theology simply becomes the humanly constructed handmaiden of our own ambitions. For Barthian Neo-orthodoxy and its cousin, postliberal theology, truth begins with God's revelation, not human imagination. Thus, it should be acknowledged that for those influenced by Barth, Kohut's views on religion may be seen as friendlier than, but just as fatal as, Ludwig Feuerbach's and Freud's views. Barth would no doubt suggest that Kohut's view of humanity is a large improvement to that of Freud, but that theology has its own tasks and purposes which are quite dif-ferent than psychoanalytic inquiry. Stated more directly, Barthians see God as "wholly other" to avoid the possibility that our image of God is nothing more than an extension of ourselves. Testing theology's claims on the basis of how it benefits humanity would be seen as a perversion of the mission of theology. And evaluating religion on the basis of how well it meets human needs would be viewed as idolatry. In other words, this view would echo Barth's ongoing concern that theology has become merely "code" for psychology. Some theologians would insist on asking, "Do theological symbols point toward anything transcendent?" More specifically, does theological language point to anything beyond the in-ner terrain of the psyche? If theological language never points beyond the world of everyday reality to a transcendent source, these critics would say, then why would we continue to use the word "theology"? Let's simply call it our "psychological imagination."

Perhaps most of the theologians interested in psychology and psy-chotherapy are more influenced by a Tillichian correlational model or even a revised correlational model (David Tracy) than a Barthian per-spective. For these individuals, theology can greatly benefit from pay-ing attention to the human sciences. As Don Browning puts it, for these individuals "psychotherapy might have something important to say to theology in its attempt to give precise, systematic articulation to the nature of God's healing and saving activity."[15] Kohut's identification of basic human needs offers guidance concerning *how* theological convictions are conveyed as well as *how* they support human flourishing. Theology and psychology can mutually teach and benefit each other. It is not the case that theology authoritatively informs psychology about the human condition and has little to learn from psychology. Instead, psychology can help further refine and illuminate theological concepts as well.

Considered in this light, experience-distant theologies, sermons, and religious practices have been frequently unresponsive to human needs. Experience-distant quarreling about highly detailed and largely insignificant theological trivia continues to push people toward a greater lack of responsiveness to each other. Experience-distant formalities that no longer speak to the human heart are leaving many pews empty. Experience-distant and emotionally non-responsive hospital visits are leaving the sick feeling disconnected. Experience-distant references to the Divine leave us with a cold, detached, fearful image of a God who warms no one's heart. Experience-distant pastoral counseling dispenses formulaic Bible verses or offers well-meaning but uninformed, even potentially disturbing, theological advice.

Religion "through the Backdoor"

Kohut would no doubt claim that he is not a theologian. And some would argue that it is unfair to try to turn him into one. Yet as Don Browning and Terry Cooper have argued, there is a quasi-theological dimension to any perspective that makes assumptions about the ultimate context of our lives, what gives us meaning, and how we should go about the task of living.[16] Or to follow the earlier work of Browning and Thomas Oden in their discussion of Carl Rogers, Kohut is making ontological assumptions about the nature of human acceptance, our dignity and value in the midst of a vast universe, and the importance of empathic immersion in each other's experience.[17] So in this sense, Kohut is *already functioning* as a philosopher and crypto-theologian as well as a psychoanalyst. And interestingly, Kohut, in one of his most revealing comments throughout the interviews, *acknowledges this*. This admission emerges in his comments about how many psychoanalysts rejected religion but seemed to turn Freudianism into a religion.

I believe, however, that seen in the *broadest* possible way, no one can do and does do without religion in one form or another. I don't mean it in terms of organized religion. I don't mean it in terms of social institutions. But I would say, for example, that psychoanalysis has more than its share of being a religion, and I think that what is wrong with psychoanalysis in that respect is really the counterpoint of Freud's attack on religion. By trying to dispense totally with even accepting religion as a powerful and meaningful and value force in human life, it came in as it were through the back door; so that instead of its being only a search for psychological truth, it became burdened with a sense of, what should I say, excessive loyalty to the originator, to the founder of psychoanalysis, to certain maxims that he held, instead of the mere gratitude and admiration for a great scientist and now let's go on from there.[18]

Kohut's notion here that denied religion will nevertheless come in "through the back door" is very noteworthy. This comment seems to signal a human need to both elevate something to the status of ultimacy and to operate on the basis of a profound loyalty to this sense of ultimacy. Paul Tillich would no doubt add that everyone operates with an ultimate concern. The issue then becomes what is truly worthy of our ultimate concern. Kohut comes close to suggesting here that adoration and radical devotion to a finite, limited source can lead to idolatry rather than greater expansion of spirit. Freud was a great and insightful person, a near-genius from whom we can learn much. But Freud did not offer the final solution to the human dilemma. He deserves our respect but not our worship. It is the nature of life to progress and move forward.

Rather interestingly, Kohut does not seem interested in a religion that attempts to do away with the concept of God. God represents the idealizing of something near perfection, our deep need to feel uplifted and connected to that which is more powerful than we are. We have a need to merge with God, to feel connected to God's stabilizing power. Kohut refers to the God concept as "an expression of the recognition that there is something about this world in our experience that does lift us up beyond the simplicity of an individual existence, that lifts us into something higher, enduring, or as I would rather say, timeless."[19]

Human Connection and Community

Kohut helps us recognize the enormous importance of life-giving, nourishing relationships in our lives. These essential others help hold the self together. Isolated people are fragmenting people. We are simply not built to be lone rangers.

> In the view of self psychology, man lives in a matrix of selfobjects from birth to death. He needs selfobjects for his psychological survival, just as he needs oxygen in his environment throughout his life for physiological survival. Certainly, the individual is exposed to the anxiety and guilt of unsolvable conflict and to the miseries of lowered self-esteem following his realization that he has failed to reach his aims or live up to his ideals. But so long as he feels that he is surrounded by selfobjects and feels reassured by their presence—either by their direct responses to him or, on the basis of past experiences, via his confidence in their lasting concern—even conflict, failure, and defeat will not destroy his self, however great his suffering may be. Self psychology does not view the essence of man's development as a move from dependence to independence, from merger to autonomy, or even as a move from no-self to self. . . . If we accept the presence of a milieu of responsive selfobjects as a necessary precondition of psychological life, if moreover, we acknowledge the fact that a healthy, normal human being is psychologically constituted in such a way that he survives only in such a milieu and is equipped with the ability to search for and find such a milieu, then our outlook on man—on his psychopathology and on his behavior in the social and historical arena—will be determined by this basic assumption.[20]

This emphasis on the significance of selfobjects helps us understand the dangers of a disengaged, disconnected religiosity, a kind of me-and-God-against-the-world mindset. We are sustained by others, or as Rabbi Harold Kushner frequently said, "Human beings are God's language." We do not have a sense of self without the support of an empathic environment. In fact, the complete withdrawal of all human responsiveness would, indeed, be hell.

Thus, perhaps many of us have chased a fictitious version of individuality and autonomy. The answer to frustrating, injurious, and wounding relationships is not to seek an unrealistic autonomy that transcends a need for relationships. Injuries are healed and the self is restored through grace-filled, responsive others who offer an empathic response to who we are. The need for recognition and affirmation is not some carry-over problem from childhood that should have been resolved long ago. It is an adult need also. If we are broken through relationships, we need to be healed through relationships. Thinkers as diverse as St. Paul and Jung have agreed that no one can boast of truly accepting him/herself in isolation. Thus, clearly, a standard of mature and healthy religious commitment is the extent to which our faith connects us, rather than isolates us, from the human community and its need for empathic responsiveness.

END NOTES

1. Kohut, First Interview, 146.
2. Kohut, Second Interview, 134.
3. Kohut, First Interview, 147.
4. Kohut, Second Interview, 134.
5. Kohut, First Interview, 117.
6. Ibid., 120.
7. Kohut, Second Interview, 148.
8. Kohut, First Interview. 116.
9. Kohut, Second Interview. 134.
10. Ibid., 128.
11. For a quick awareness of theology's abundant wrestling with the subject-object issue, look up "subject-object in theology" on the Internet.
12. Randall, "Legacy of Kohut for Religion and Psychology."
13. Quoted in Erikson, *Young Man Luther*, 251.
14. Kohut, First Interview, 136.
15. Browning, *Atonement and Psychotherapy*, 26–27.
16. Browning and Cooper, *Religious Thought and the Modern Psychologies*.
17. Browning, *Atonement and Psychotherapy*; Oden, *Kerygma and Counseling*.
18. Kohut, First Interview, 116.
19. Kohut, Second Interview, 128.
20. Kohut, "Reflections on Advances in Self Psychology," 478–81.

Closing Words for Our Readers

B Y NOW YOU LIKELY understand how every human act is received by an individual as a self-selfobject experience. Beneath apparently objective and detached engagements and conversations, the individual is constantly attuned to how others (as selfobjects) are supportive or non-supportive of his or her self. Every human interaction becomes a self-selfobject experience—more or less recognized by the individual but inevitably shaping how the individual feels about his or her self and even about life in general.

Narcissistic sensitivities (sensitivities to being injured) are especially heightened during moments of transition, such as greetings and goodbyes. A great party can be marred for us if we feel that the host or others have just waved perfunctorily at us when we leave, rather than overtly showing that they have enjoyed being with us and will miss us when we're gone. How we greet others and how we say goodbye have marked impact upon the well-being of a person, especially if the person's self has been weakened and left fragmentation-prone by past narcissistic injuries. You can imagine, therefore, how narcissistically potent are those first greetings between the new pastor and the new church, and how the acts of goodbye between the leaving pastor and the parish left can be either narcissistic blessings or narcissistic curses With this in mind, allow us to express to you a warm goodbye as you leave our time together.

While we have endeavored to be an available selfobject for you in this particular context, we also acknowledge that you have also been an imagined selfobject for us. We experience a certain enhancement of pride as we picture you spending time reading these pages, perhaps occasionally benefiting from an insight, perhaps even utilizing it in your own work. While your criticisms of our work will inevitably prick our self-esteem to some degree, they will not severely disrupt our self cohesion. And so we welcome your comments that may question all or part of our presentation here, believing that this will facilitate our own efforts to free, exercise, and broaden our capacities for empathic understanding and responding.

Terry D. Cooper – tcooper@stlcc.edu
Robert L. Randall – rrandall42@gmail.com

Bibliography

Augustine of Hippo. *The City of God*. Translated by Henry Bettenson. New York: Penguin, 1972.

Browning, Don S. *Atonement and Psychotherapy*. Philadelphia: Westminster, 1966.

———. *A Fundamental Practical Theology: Descriptive and Strategic Proposals*. Minneapolis: Fortress, 1991.

Browning, Don S., and Terry D. Cooper. *Religious Thought and the Modern Psychologies*. 2nd ed. Minneapolis: Fortress, 2004.

Burns, J. Patout, editor and translator. *Theological Anthropology*. Sources of Early Christian Thought. Philadelphia: Fortress, 1981.

Capps, Donald. *Deadly Sins and Saving Virtues*. Philadelphia: Fortress, 1987.

———. *The Depleted Self: Sin in a Narcissistic Age*. Minneapolis: Fortress, 1993.

Cooper, Terry D. *Reinhold Niebuhr and Psychology: The Ambiguities of the Self*. Macon, GA: Mercer University Press, 2009.

Dobson, Marcia. "Freud, Kohut, Sophocles: Did Oedipus Do Wrong?" Paper presented at the 29th Annual International Conference on the Psychology of the Self, Chicago, October 26–29, 2006.

Erikson, Erik H. *Young Man Luther: A Study in Psychoanalysis and History*. New York: Norton, 1958.

Freud, Sigmund. *Civilization and Its Discontents*. Translated by James Strachey. New York: Norton, 1961.

———. *The Interpretation of Dreams*. The Standard Edition of the Complete Psychological Works of Sigmund Freud, vols. 4–5. London: Hogarth, 1953–.

Gay, Volney Patrick. *Understanding the Occult: Fragmentation and Repair of the Self*. Minneapolis: Fortress, 1989.

Greenlee, Lynn F., Jr. "Kohut's Self Psychology and Theory of Narcissism: Some Implications Regarding the Fall and Restoration of Humanity." *Journal of Psychology and Theology* 14.2 (1986) 110–16.

Homans, Peter. *The Ability to Mourn: Disillusionment and the Social Origins of Psychoanalysis*. Chicago: University of Chicago Press, 1989.

Kernberg, Otto F. *Borderline Conditions and Pathological Narcissism*. Classical Psychoanalysis and Its Applications. New York: J. Aronson, 1975.

Kohut, Heinz. *The Analysis of the Self: A Systematic Approach to the Psychoanalytic Treatment of Narcissistic Personality Disorders*. New York: International Universities Press, 1971.

———. *The Chicago Institute Lectures*. Edited by Paul and Marion Tolpin. Hillsdale, NJ: Analytic Press, 1996.

———. "Forms and Transformations of Narcissism." In *The Search for the Self: Selected Writings of Heinz Kohut*, edited by Paul H. Ornstein, 1:454. New York: International Universities Press, 1978.

————. "Introspection, Empathy, and Psychoanalysis: An Examination of the Relationship Between Modes of Observation and Theory." In *The Search for the Self: Selected Writings of Heinz Kohut*, edited by Paul H. Ornstein, 1:205–32. New York: International Universities Press, 1978.

————. "Introspection, Empathy, and the Semicircle of Mental Health." In *The Search for the Self: Selected Writings of Heinz Kohut*, edited by Paul H. Ornstein, 4:537–67. New York: International Universities Press, 1991.

————. *The Kohut Seminars on Self Psychology and Psychotherapy with Adolescents and Young Adults*. Edited by Mariam Elson. New York: Norton, 1987.

————. "Reflections on Advances in Self Psychology." In *Advances in Self Psychology*, edited by Arnold Goldberg, 478–81. New York: International Universities Press, 1980.

————. *Self Psychology and the Humanities: Reflections on a New Psychoanalytic Approach*. Edited by Charles B. Strozier. New York: Norton, 1985.

Levin, Jerome D. *Treatment of Alcoholism and Other Addictions: A Self Psychology Approach*. Northvale, NJ: J. Aronson, 1987.

Miller, Jule P. *Using Self Psychology in Child Psychotherapy: The Restoration of the Child*. Northvale, NJ: J. Aaronson, 1996.

Mitchell, Stephen A., and Margaret J. Black. *Freud and Beyond: A History of Modern Psychoanalytic Thought*. New York: Basic Books, 1995.

Niebuhr, Reinhold. "Human Creativity and Self-Concern in Freud's Thought." In *Freud and the 20th Century*, edited by Benjamin Nelson, 259–76. New York: Meridian, 1957.

Oden, Thomas C. *Kerygma and Counseling: Toward a Covenant Ontology for Secular Psychotherapy*. Philadelphia: Westminster, 1966.

Randall, Robert L. "The Legacy of Kohut for Religion and Psychology." *Journal of Religion and Psychological Health* 23.2 (November 1984) 106–14.

————. "Soteriological Dimensions in the Work of Heinz Kohut." *Journal of Religion and Health* 19.2 (Summer 1980) 83–91.

Ricoeur, Paul. *The Symbolism of Evil*. Boston: Beacon, 1967.

Rowe, Crayton E., and David S. MacIsaac. *Empathic Attunement: The "Technique" of Psychoanalytic Self Psychology*. Northvale, NJ: J. Aronson, 1989.

Schimmel, Solomon. *The Seven Deadly Sins: Jewish, Christian, and Classical Reflections on Human Psychology*. New York: Oxford University Press, 1997.

Strozier, Charles B. *Heinz Kohut: The Making of a Psychoanalyst*. New York: Other Press, 2001.

————. "Heinz Kohut's Struggles with Religion, Ethnicity, and God." In *Religion, Society, and Psychoanalysis: Readings in Contemporary Theory*, edited by Janet Liebman Jacobs and Donald Capps, 165–80. Boulder, CO: Westview, 1997.

Tillich, Paul. "The Impact of Pastoral Counseling on Theological Thought." In *The Ministry and Mental Health*, edited by Hans Hofman, 15. New York: Association Press, 1960.

————. "The Theological Significance of Existentialism and Psychoanalysis." In *The Meaning of Health: Essays in Existentialism, Psychoanalysis, and Religion*, by Paul Tillich, edited by Perry LeFevre, 81–95. Chicago: Exploration, 1984.

Watts, Alan. *Beyond Theology: The Art of Godmanship*. New York: Vintage, 1973.

Weatherhead, Leslie Dixon. *The Christian Agnostic*. Nashville: Abingdon, 1965.

65263444R00100

Made in the USA
Lexington, KY
09 July 2017